THE BILINGUAL SERI
THE MOST IMPRESSIVE BEAU

最美中国双语系列

民俗文化

FOLK CULTURE

主　编◎青　闰
副主编◎郝雅文　陈　旗
参　编◎薛茜茜　赵　雷　姚春立

中国科学技术大学出版社

内 容 简 介

"最美中国双语系列"是一套精品文化推广图书,包括《风景名胜》《民俗文化》《饮食文化》《杰出人物》《科技成就》《中国故事》六册,旨在传播中华优秀文化,传承中华民族宝贵的民族精神,展示奋进中的最美中国,可供广大中华文化爱好者、英语学习者及外国友人参考使用。

本书介绍了中国一些具有代表性的民俗文化,有助于读者了解中国的民乐、书画、建筑、服饰等艺术及传统节日等习俗。

图书在版编目(CIP)数据

民俗文化:英汉对照/青闻主编. —合肥:中国科学技术大学出版社,2021.11
(最美中国双语系列)
ISBN 978-7-312-05229-3

Ⅰ.民… Ⅱ.青… Ⅲ.风俗习惯—介绍—中国—英、汉 Ⅳ.K892

中国版本图书馆CIP数据核字(2021)第120548号

民俗文化
MINSU WENHUA

出版	中国科学技术大学出版社 安徽省合肥市金寨路96号,230026 http://press.ustc.edu.cn https://zgkxjsdxcbs.tmall.com
印刷	安徽国文彩印有限公司
发行	中国科学技术大学出版社
经销	全国新华书店
开本	880 mm×1230 mm 1/32
印张	8.25
字数	200千
版次	2021年11月第1版
印次	2021年11月第1次印刷
定价	35.00元

前言 Preface

文化是一个国家与民族的灵魂。"最美中国双语系列"旨在弘扬和推广中华优秀文化,突出文化鲜活主题,彰显文化核心理念,挖掘文化内在元素,拓展文化宽广视野,为广大读者了解、体验和传播中华文化精髓提供全新的视角。本系列图书秉持全面、凝练、准确、实用、自然、流畅的撰写原则,全方位、多层面、多角度地展现中华文化的源远流长和博大精深,对于全民文化素质的提升具有独特的现实意义,同时也为世界文化的互联互通提供必要的借鉴和可靠的参考。

"最美中国双语系列"包括《风景名胜》《民俗文化》《饮食文化》《杰出人物》《科技成就》《中国故事》六册,每册中的各篇文章以文化剪影为主线,以佳句点睛、情景对话和生词注解为副线,别出心裁,精彩呈现中华文化的方方面面。

"最美中国双语系列"充分体现以读者为中心的编写理念,从文化剪影到生词注解,读者可由简及繁、由繁及精、由精及思地感知中华文化的独特魅力。书中的主线和副线是一体两面的有机结合,不可分割,如果说主线是灵魂,副线则是灵魂的眼睛。

"最美中国双语系列"的推出,是讲好中国故事、展现中国立场、传播中国文化的一道盛宴,读者可以从中感悟生活。

《民俗文化》包括戏曲与民乐、书画与手工艺、建筑、服饰、节日与节气、技艺六部分,这里有历史悠久的戏剧、民族乐器、皮影戏,有精

雕细琢的书法、国画、篆刻、刺绣、陶瓷、泥塑、剪纸,有独一无二的宫殿、园林、传统民居,也有别具风韵的旗袍、汉服,还有独具特色的春节、元宵节、端午节、七夕节、中秋节、二十四节气……可谓应有尽有,精彩纷呈。

本书由江苏省镇江第一中学郝雅文、郑州西亚斯学院陈旗撰写初稿,郑州郑东新区龙翔学校薛茜茜、焦作大学赵雷撰写二稿,焦作大学姚春立撰写三稿,焦作大学青闰负责全书统稿与定稿。

最后,在本书即将付梓之际,衷心感谢中国科学技术大学出版社的大力支持,感谢朋友们的一路陪伴,感谢家人们始终不渝的鼓励和支持。

青 闰

2021年3月6日

目 录 Contents

前言 Preface ·· i

第一部分　戏曲与民乐
Part I　Operas and Folk Music

京剧　Peking Opera ·································· 003
昆曲　Kun Opera ····································· 008
越剧　Yue Opera ····································· 012
黄梅戏　Huangmei Opera ························· 015
评剧　Ping Opera ···································· 018
豫剧　Yu Opera ······································ 022
编钟　Chime Bells ·································· 027
古琴　Guqin ··· 031
古筝　Guzheng ······································ 035
琵琶　Pipa ··· 040
二胡　Erhu ·· 043
箫　Xiao ··· 047
锣鼓　Gongs and Drums ··························· 050

第二部分　书画与手工艺
Part II　Calligraphy, Painting and Handicrafts

书法　Calligraphy ···057

中国画　Traditional Chinese Painting ···············062

篆刻　Seal Cutting ···067

刺绣　Embroidery ··072

陶瓷　Ceramics ··077

剪纸　Paper-cut ··082

印染　Printing and Dyeing ································087

景泰蓝　Cloisonné ···092

中国结　Chinese Knot ······································097

风筝　Kites ··102

第三部分　建　筑
Part III　Architecture

宫殿　Palace ··109

园林　Gardens ···114

北京四合院　Beijing Siheyuan ·························119

上海里弄　Shanghai Lilong ······························123

客家土楼　Hakka Tulou ···································127

目录

第四部分　服　饰
Part IV　Dress

旗袍　Cheongsam ·· 135

汉服　Hanfu ··· 140

少数民族服饰　Costumes of the Ethnic Minorities ··············· 145

第五部分　节日与节气
Part V　Festivals and Solar Terms

春节　Spring Festival ··· 153

元宵节　Lantern Festival ·· 158

清明节　Qingming Festival ·· 163

端午节　Dragon Boat Festival ····································· 168

七夕节　Qixi Festival ··· 174

中秋节　Mid-Autumn Festival ····································· 179

重阳节　Double Ninth Festival ···································· 184

二十四节气　Twenty-Four Solar Terms ··························· 189

V

第六部分 技 艺
Part VI Skills

中医　Traditional Chinese Medicine ·······················197

茶艺　Tea Ceremony ·····································203

武术　Wushu ··209

杂技　Acrobatics ···215

围棋　Go ···221

相声　Crosstalk ··227

秧歌　Yangko ···232

高跷　Stilts ··235

腰鼓舞　Waist Drum Dance ·····························239

皮影戏　Shadow Puppetry ······························244

泥塑　Clay Sculpture ·····································249

老北京兔儿爷　Old Beijing Rabbit Figurine ···············252

第一部分　戏曲与民乐

Part I Operas and Folk Music

京剧

Peking Opera

 导入语　Lead-in

京剧,原称"皮黄"或"京调",是中国传统文化的结晶,被誉为中国的"国粹"。京剧脸谱分为整脸、英雄脸、六分脸、歪脸、神仙脸和丑角脸等。京剧音乐属于板腔体,主要唱腔有二黄和西皮,常用唱腔有南梆子、四平调、高拨子、反二黄、娃娃调和吹腔。京剧早期分为生、旦、净、末、丑、武行、流行(龙套),后来归为生、旦、净、丑。京剧融合了中国南北方戏曲元素,通过丰富多样的艺术表现手段,彰显了中国传统文化的博大精深和独特魅力。京剧的分布以北京为中心,遍及中国,是介绍、传播中国传统艺术文化的重要媒介。梅兰芳是卓越的京剧表演艺术家之一,代表剧目有《宇宙锋》《霸王别姬》《贵妃醉酒》《穆桂英挂帅》等。

文化剪影 Cultural Outline

Peking Opera is the **crystallization**① of various Chinese opera art forms, with a history of more than 200 years, known as the **quintessence**② of China. With its unique artistic form, it mainly deals with historical themes, which is highly appreciated and loved by the audience and has an **unprecedented**③ impact on the development of Chinese artistic culture.

京剧是中国各种戏曲艺术形式的结晶，具有两百多年的历史，被誉为中国的"国粹"。京剧艺术形式独特，主要讲述历史题材，深受观众的赞赏和喜爱，对中国艺术文化的发展具有空前的影响。

Peking Opera is a form of expression of traditional Chinese drama, showing an **encyclopedia**④ of Chinese culture to the audience through fascinating stories, delicate paintings, **exquisite**⑤ costumes, graceful gestures, **acrobatic**⑥ martial arts and other **comprehensive**⑦ performing arts.

京剧是中国传统戏剧的一种表现形式，它也是一本关于中国文化的百科全书，各观众展现了引人入胜的故事、精致的油彩、精美的服装、优美的手势和杂技武打等综合表演艺术。

Peking Opera is regarded as a comprehensive performing art with techniques such as singing, acting, recitation and acrobatics, the audience can **distinguish**⑧ the good and evil of characters through the classification of facial makeup, which can be said to be a unique element of the Chinese Peking Opera stage.

京剧被视为一门综合性表演艺术,采用念、唱、做、打等技巧。观众可以通过脸谱的不同来区分人物的善恶,可以说脸谱是中国京剧舞台特有的元素。

佳句点睛 Punchlines

1. Peking Opera is an important medium of introducing and spreading the traditional Chinese culture.

京剧是介绍和传播中国传统文化的一种重要媒介。

2. Peking Opera is regarded as the quintessence of Chinese culture, its themes focusing on the performance of historical stories.

京剧被誉为中国的"国粹",主要表演历史题材的故事。

3. Peking Opera is an **integrated**⑨ performance art and the harmonious combination of many local art forms.

京剧是一种综合表演艺术,是诸多地方艺术形式的有机组合。

情景对话 Situational Dialogue

A: Hi, Linda. How do you spend your weekend?

B: Hi, Helen. I wanna see *Farewell, My Concubine* this weekend. Have you seen it?

A: Yes. I saw it last week. The film is so wonderful that it is worth seeing.

B: Really? I've heard that there are some Peking Opera performances in the movie. Peking Opera is the essence of Chinese culture. I love traditional Chinese culture very much. Can you tell me about Peking Opera?

A: Sure. Peking Opera is the integrated performance art and the harmonious combination of many local art forms. In addition, the audience can distinguish the good and evil through the **classification**① of Peking opera masks, which are unique elements of Chinese Peking opera stage.

B: Bravo! I can't wait to see it now.

A: 你好,琳达,周末你怎么安排啊?

B: 你好,海伦,我想去看《霸王别姬》。你看过吗?

A: 我上周看过了。电影非常精彩,值得一看。

B: 真的吗?我听说电影里有一些京剧表演,京剧是中国的"国粹",我非常喜爱中国传统文化。你能给我讲讲京剧吗?

A: 当然可以。京剧是一种综合表演艺术,是很多地方艺术形式的有机结合。另外,观众可以通过脸谱的不同来辨别忠奸善恶,脸谱是中国京剧舞台特有的元素。

B: 你讲得太棒了!我现在就迫不及待想看了。

生词注解 Notes

① crystallization /ˌkrɪstəlaɪˈzeɪʃn/   n. 结晶化；具体化

② quintessence /kwɪnˈtesns/   n. 精华；精髓

③ unprecedented /ʌnˈpresɪdentɪd/   adj. 空前的；前所未有的

④ encyclopedia /ɪnˌsaɪkləˈpiːdɪə/   n. 百科全书

⑤ exquisite /ɪkˈskwɪzɪt/   adj. 精美的；雅致的

⑥ acrobatic /ˌækrəˈbætɪk /   adj. 杂技的；杂技演员的

⑦ comprehensive /ˌkɒmprɪˈhensɪv /   adj. 综合性的；全部的

⑧ distinguish /dɪˈstɪŋgwɪʃ/   vt. 区分；辨别

⑨ integrated /ˈɪntɪgreɪtɪd/   adj. 综合的；完整的

⑩ classification /ˌklæsɪfɪˈkeɪʃn/   n. 分类；类别

昆曲

Kun Opera

导入语 Lead-in

昆曲是中国古老的戏曲剧种之一，原称"昆腔""昆剧"，由元朝末期昆山人顾坚所创。明朝嘉靖年间，昆曲家魏良辅对昆山腔进行了重大改革，吸收了当时受欢迎的海盐腔、余姚腔和弋阳腔的特点，形成了婉转优美的"水磨调"，即今天的昆曲。昆曲是中国汉族传统戏曲艺术中的珍品，被誉为"百花园中的一朵兰花"。昆曲表演具有行腔婉转、舞蹈性强、动作细腻优美等特点，通过欣赏昆曲的精湛表演，观众可以领略到中国地方戏曲文化的独特魅力。此外，昆曲还创造了中国戏曲史上最完整的民族戏曲表演体系，对许多地方戏曲剧种产生了深远影响，被称为"百戏之祖"，享有"中国戏曲之母"的美誉。2001年，昆曲被联合国教科文组织评为"人类口述和非物质遗产代表作"，2006年被国务院列入《第一批国家级非物质文化遗产名录》。

 ## 文化剪影　Cultural Outline

Kun Opera, which **originated**① from the early stage of Chinese folk opera in Kunshan, Jiangsu, is the mother of traditional Chinese operas and one of the old forms of Chinese operas with a history of over six hundred years. Kun Opera is honored as the "**orchid**② in the garden of flowers", which has the greatest influence on the traditional Chinese dramatic art.

昆曲是一种起源于江苏昆山早期的民间戏曲，是中国传统戏曲之母，也是中国古老的戏曲形式之一，至今已有六百多年的历史。昆曲被誉为"百花园中的兰花"，对中国传统戏剧艺术影响最大。

Kun Opera combines poetic context, musical **melody**③, dancing movements and dramatic performances, showing a splendid and magical traditional Chinese culture. The most well-known representative plays are *The Peony Pavilion*, *The West Chamber*, *The Palace of Eternal Youth*, and so on.

昆曲融合了诗情画意、音乐旋律、舞蹈动作和戏剧表演，展现了灿烂而神奇的中国传统文化。最著名的代表剧目有《牡丹亭》《西厢记》《长生殿》等。

Kun Opera has developed into present Kunshan Operatic Tune through absorbing and combining the essence and strengths of four operatic tunes—Haiyan Operatic Tune, Yuyao Operatic Tune, Yiyang Operatic Tune and Kunshan Operatic Tune—in the Ming Dynasty. Kun Opera performances have the unique characteristics of beautiful modeling, light and flexible dance movements, and delicate and **lyrical**[④] movements.

昆曲是在吸收和结合明代四大声腔——海盐腔、余姚腔、戈阳腔和昆山腔的精髓和长处的基础上发展起来的。昆曲表演具有造型优美、舞姿轻盈灵动和动作细腻抒情的特点。

佳句点睛　Punchlines

1. Kun Opera is honored as "The Mother of Chinese Operas".
昆曲被誉为"中国戏曲之母"。

2. Kun Opera has produced a large number of well-known plays, showcasing the brilliant and magical traditional Chinese culture.
昆曲有大量家喻户晓的剧作,展示了灿烂而神奇的中国传统文化。

3. Kun Opera embodies the beauty of simplicity, **connotation**[⑤] and wisdom of Chinese national culture with its elegant style and exquisite lyric movements.

昆曲以优美的风格和细腻的抒情动作体现了中华民族文化的朴素美、内涵美和智慧美。

 生词注解 Notes

① originate /əˈrɪdʒɪneɪt/　*vi.* 发源；起源

② orchid /ˈɔːkɪd/　*n.* 兰花；兰科植物

③ melody /ˈmelədɪ/　*n.* 旋律；曲调

④ lyrical /ˈlɪrɪkl/　*adj.* 抒情诗调的；感情丰富的

⑤ connotation /ˌkɒnəˈteɪʃn/　*n.* 含义；内涵

越剧

Yue Opera

 导入语 Lead-in

越剧诞生于20世纪初,初称"小歌班"或"的笃班",前身是清朝道光末年浙江嵊州一带流行的说唱艺术——落地唱书。1916年进入上海,受到绍剧和京剧的影响,越剧有了较大发展,被称为"绍兴文戏"。20世纪30年代,形成了全部由女演员演出的"女子文戏",同时受话剧和昆曲影响,歌舞并重,1938年始称越剧。新中国成立后,越剧恢复了男女合演,著名演员有袁雪芬等。越剧表演以唱为主,美妙动听,抒情温婉,故事主题多以"才子佳人"为主。越剧被称为"流传最广的地方剧种",有"第二国剧"之称,2006年被国务院列入《第一批国家级非物质文化遗产名录》。

文化剪影 Cultural Outline

Yue Opera is one of the five major national operas in China, with a history of more than one hundred years. It is popular in East China such as Zhejiang and Shanghai, enjoying a high reputation among a wide range of audience.

越剧是中国五大民族戏曲之一,已有一百多年的历史,在浙江、上海等华东地区广受欢迎,并在广大观众中享有盛誉。

Influenced by various opera forms such as Peking Opera and Kun Opera, Yue Opera has made great progress and developed into a singing and dancing style in which actors and actresses perform together. Among them, Yuan Xuefen is a **household**[①] name. Its representative plays are *The Peacock Flies Southeast*, *The Butterfly Lovers*, and so on.

受京剧和昆曲等多种戏曲形式的影响,越剧取得了长足的进步,发展成为男女演员共同表演的歌舞风格,其中袁雪芬是家喻户晓的代表演员。越剧代表剧目有《孔雀东南飞》和《梁山伯与祝英台》等。

Yue Opera highlights the delicate and elegant spirit of the south of the Yangtze River with vivid and touching performances and **amazing**[②] beautiful voices. The theme of Yue Opera is mainly "talented scholars and beautiful ladies". It is said to be the most popular local opera, known as "the second national opera".

越剧以生动感人的表演和令人惊叹的优美唱腔彰显了江南细腻典雅的精神风貌。越剧的主题主要是"才子佳人"。据说越剧是最受欢迎的地方戏,被誉为"第二国剧"。

佳句点睛　Punchlines

1. Yue Opera has won the love of the broad masses of people with its elegence and delicacy.

越剧以高雅细腻的特点赢得了广大人民的喜爱。

2. Yue Opera displays the brilliance and unique charm of traditional Chinese local art.

越剧展现了中国传统地方艺术的辉煌和独特魅力。

3. Yue Opera, with its theme focusing on "talented scholars and beautiful ladies", is full of the spiritual characteristics of brightness, softness and sweetness of the south of the Yangtze River.

越剧主要以"才子佳人"为主题,富有江南明媚柔美的精神特色。

生词注解　Notes

① household /ˈhaʊshəʊld/　*adj.* 家喻户晓的

② amazing /əˈmeɪzɪŋ/　*adj.* 惊艳的;令人惊诧的

黄梅戏

Huangmei Opera

 导入语　Lead-in

　　黄梅戏最早可以追溯到唐朝,形成于清朝乾隆末期,是由湖北黄梅的采茶调传入安徽安庆一带后逐步发展而成的。黄梅戏唱腔淳朴流畅,富有表现力,以花腔、彩腔和主腔三种唱法为主,具有浓郁的乡土风味和生活气息。黄梅戏演员严凤英在唱腔和表演方面取得了突出成就,为黄梅戏的传播和发展做出了重要贡献。黄梅戏经过不断改革和创新,不仅丰富了地方传统戏曲艺术文化,也引领了中国地方戏曲的前沿发展,留下了许多经典名作,如《天仙配》《女驸马》等。2006年,黄梅戏被国务院列入《第一批国家级非物质文化遗产名录》。2009年,中国首个以戏剧为主题的国家级戏剧博物馆——中国黄梅戏博物馆在安徽安庆落成。

文化剪影 Cultural Outline

Huangmei Opera, formerly known as "tea-picking tune," has a history of more than two hundred years. It is said to have first appeared in Huangmei County, Hubei Province, and **flourished**[①] in Anqing City, Anhui Province and many surrounding provinces. At present, Huangmei Opera has become a kind of entertainment, and it is one of the influential operas in China.

黄梅戏,原名"采茶调",具有两百多年的历史,据说最初出现在湖北省黄梅县,并在安徽省安庆市及周边许多省份蓬勃发展。目前,黄梅戏已经成为一种娱乐活动,是中国极具影响力的戏曲之一。

Huangmei Opera is mainly composed of three singing styles such as color tune, **coloratura**[②] and main tune, fully displaying its **inherent**[③] charm and characteristics. The representative works are *The Fairy Couple*, *The Female Consort Prince*, and so on.

黄梅戏以彩腔、花腔、主腔三种唱法为主,充分展现了黄梅戏的内在魅力和特性,代表剧目有《天仙配》《女驸马》等。

Huangmei Opera is simple in costume, lyric in melody, plain in language, distinctive in local characteristics, beautiful in **timbre**[④] and fascinating.

黄梅戏服装朴实,曲调抒情,语言质朴,地方特色鲜明,音色优美,引人入胜。

佳句点睛 Punchlines

1. Huangmei Opera is a kind of opera with strong local characteristics.

黄梅戏是一种具有浓郁地方特色的戏曲。

2. Huangmei Opera showcases the inner essence of the traditional Chinese local operas.

黄梅戏展示了中国传统戏曲的内在精髓。

3. Huangmei Opera presents the unique charm and value of Chinese national culture.

黄梅戏展现了中国民族文化的独特魅力和价值。

生词注解 Notes

① flourish /ˈflʌrɪʃ/ vi. 繁荣；茁壮成长
② coloratura /ˌkɒlərəˈtʊərə/ n. 花腔
③ inherent /ɪnˈherənt/ adj. 固有的；内在的
④ timbre /ˈtæmbə(r)/ n. 音色；音质

评剧

Ping Opera

导入语　Lead-in

评剧流行于华北和东北一带，前身是19世纪末河北小曲"对口莲花落"。作为穷人行乞的演唱艺术，莲花落表演的内容常为说唱吉祥如意的话或演唱故事。20世纪30年代，评剧又被称为"蹦蹦戏""平腔梆子戏""奉天落子"和"评戏"等。1935年，老艺术家吕海寰建议改名为"评剧"，寓意"评古论今"。评剧的艺术特征主要表现为以唱功见长，吐字清晰，唱词浅显易懂，贴近生活，表演形式活泼自由，深受广大观众喜欢。代表作有《小二黑结婚》等。著名演员有小白玉霜、新凤霞等。2006年，评剧被国务院列入《第一批国家级非物质文化遗产名录》。

文化剪影 Cultural Outline

Ping Opera, short for "Bengbengxi" "Laozixi" or "Pingxi" originated in the rural areas in the eastern Hebei Province with a history of less than one hundred years. Lyu Haihuan, an elderly artist, suggested in 1935 that it be changed to "Ping Opera", which means "commenting on the past and the present". Ping Opera with bamboo **clapper**① as the main accompaniment instrument is deeply loved by the masses for its unique charm.

评剧,简称"蹦蹦戏""落子戏"或"评戏",发源于冀东农村,距今不到百年,1935年老艺术家吕海寰建议将其改为"评剧",意为"评古论今"。以竹板为主要伴奏乐器的评剧因其独特的魅力而深受群众喜爱。

Ping Opera is a begging art of the poor, which **originated**② from folk songs and **ballads**③, and its performance content mainly consists of **auspicious**④ words or ballads. A great number of classic works such as *The Flower Is a Go-between, Du Shiniang*, and so on were published one after another, which have had a profound impact on the masses of the people.

评剧是穷人乞讨的一种艺术,起源于民歌民谣,其表演内容主要以吉祥词或歌谣为主。《花为媒》《杜十娘》等一大批经典名作相继问世,对人民群众产生了深远影响。

Ping Opera is characterized by **superb**⑤ singing skills, clear voice, simple lyrics and free and lively performance while its content is easy to understand, close to the people's daily life, and deeply loved by people. In 2006, it was listed as *The First* **Batch**⑥ *of National* **Intangible**⑦ *Cultural Heritage*.

评剧具有唱功精湛、声音清晰、唱词简单和表演自由活泼等特点，表演内容通俗易懂，贴近人们的日常生活，深受人们喜爱，2006年，评剧被列入《第一批国家级非物质文化遗产名录》。

佳句点睛　Punchlines

1. Ping Opera closely linked with rural life reflects locally down-to-earth life.

评剧与乡村生活紧密相连，反映了当地的现实生活。

2. Ping Opera mostly adopting auspicious words exerts profound influences on people.

评剧语言以吉祥和祝福词汇为主，对人们产生了深远的影响。

3. Ping Opera brings out typical features of Chinese national local artistic culture.

评剧呈现了中华民族地方艺术文化的典型特征。

生词注解 Notes

① clapper /ˈklæpə(r)/ *n.* 拍板；钟锤

② originate /əˈrɪdʒɪneɪt/ *v.* 起源于……；产生于……

③ ballad /ˈbæləd/ *n.* 民谣；叙事诗

④ auspicious /ɔːˈspɪʃəs/ *adj.* 吉祥的；吉利的

⑤ superb /suːˈpɜːb/ *adj.* 极好的；(信心、控制力或技巧)超凡的

⑥ batch /bætʃ/ *n.* 一批；批次

⑦ intangible /ɪnˈtændʒəbl/ *adj.* 非物质的；无形的

豫剧

Yu Opera

 导入语 Lead-in

豫剧,也称"河南梆子"或"河南高调",流行于河南及周边各省的部分地区,是陕西梆子传入河南后,同当地民歌小调结合并通过不断改革和创新发展起来的,因河南简称"豫",故称豫剧。豫剧不仅继承和发扬了中国传统戏曲艺术,还因其贴近现实、反映生活、故事性强而深受百姓喜爱。豫剧唱腔铿锵大气、抑扬顿挫、韵味醇美、生动活泼、情感丰沛,豫剧以梆子击节和板胡为主要伴奏乐器,传统剧目八百多种,经典剧目有《朝阳沟》《穆桂英挂帅》等,著名演员有马金凤、常香玉等。2006年,豫剧被国务院列入《第一批国家级非物质文化遗产名录》。

文化剪影 Cultural Outline

Yu Opera, also known as "Henan Clapper Opera" or "Henan High Tune", originated in Henan Province and its surrounding areas, is one of China's five major operas. It not only carries forward the traditional Chinese opera art, but also reflects the great achievements and wisdom of ancient artists, enjoying the nationalwide **popularity**①.

豫剧，又称"河南梆子"或"河南高调"，发源于河南省及其周边地区，是中国五大戏曲剧种之一。豫剧不仅弘扬了中国传统戏曲艺术，而且反映了古代艺术家的伟大成就和智慧，享誉全国。

There are more than eight hundred traditional plays in the repertoire of Yu Opera, among which the representative classics are *Chaoyanggou*, *Silver Spears*, *Mu Guiying Takes Command*, and so on, winning a widely **acclaimed**② reputation among the audiences. One of the **prominent**③ performing artists of Yu Opera is Chang Xiangyu, a household name in China. In 2006, Yu Opera was listed as *The First Batch*④ *of National Intangible Cultural Heritage*.

豫剧的传统剧目有八百多种，其中具有代表性的经典剧目有《朝阳沟》《对花枪》《穆桂英挂帅》等，在观众中享有盛誉。在中国家喻户晓的常香玉是杰出的豫剧表演艺术家之一。2006年，豫剧被列入《第一批国家级非物质文化遗产名录》。

The melody of Yu Opera is mainly composed of clappers and banhus. It is famous for its **sonorous**[5] **cadence**[6], mellow and lively aria, expressing characters' intense emotions and **demonstrating**[7] local distinctive artistic charm.

豫剧主要以梆子和板胡为主要伴奏乐器,以其铿锵有力、抑扬顿挫的节奏,圆润活泼的唱腔而著称,同时抒发了人物的强烈情感,展现了地方特色的艺术魅力。

 佳句点睛　Punchlines

1. Yu Opera inherits and carries forward the traditional Chinese opera art.

豫剧继承和发扬了中国传统戏曲艺术。

2. Yu Opera is warmly welcomed by the audience with a large number of widely acclaimed classics.

豫剧凭借大量广受赞誉的经典佳作受到观众的热烈欢迎。

3. Yu Opera demonstrates local distinctive artistic charm featuring strong emotion and unrestrained masculinity.

豫剧表现出了人物强烈的情感、奔放阳刚的性格,具有独特的地方艺术魅力。

情景对话 Situational Dialogue

A: Have you seen *Sing China*? I really like *Beside the Plum Tree* of Leehom Wang. Have you heard about it?

B: Surely, it's a really fabulous song. It is said to have been inspired by *The Peony Pavilion*, a masterpiece of Kun Opera from Tang Xianzu, a dramatist of the Yuan Dynasty. Kun Opera derived from the early folk operas in Kunshan, Jiangsu and is viewed as the source of many other types of traditional operas, such as Yue Opera, Huangmei Opera, Ping Opera, Yu Opera, and so on, with the reputation of "The Mother of Chinese Operas".

A: Superb! What are the representative works of other traditional operas **respectively**[①]?

B: *Chaoyanggou* and *Mu Guiying Takes Command* are representa-tive works of Yu Opera, *The Flower Is A Go-between*, and *Du Shiniang* are of Ping Opera, *The Fairy Match* and *The Female Consort Prince* are of Huangmei Opera, and *The Peacock Flying Southeast* and *The Butterfly Lovers* are of Yue Opera. All of them are classics representing the excellent traditional culture of the Chinese nation.

A: The traditional Chinese culture is profound and breathtaking. Having heard your explanation, I can't wait to appreciate it.

B: The Henan Television Station has a variety show called *Spring of the Theater*, which is a better choice for you if you wanna enjoy more about traditional Chinese opera.

A: 你看过《唱响中国》吗？我真的很喜欢王力宏的歌曲《在梅边》。你听过吗？

B: 当然听过，这是一首非常棒的歌，据说是受元代剧作家汤显祖的昆曲名作《牡丹亭》的启发而改编的。昆曲起源于江苏昆山早期的民间戏曲，被誉为粤剧、黄梅戏、评剧和豫剧等多种传统戏曲的源头，有"中国戏曲之母"的美誉。

A: 太棒了！其他传统戏曲的代表作分别是什么呢？

B: 豫剧代表作有《朝阳沟》和《穆桂英挂帅》，评剧代表作有《花为媒》和《杜十娘》，《天仙配》和《女驸马》是黄梅戏的代表作，《孔雀东南飞》和《梁山伯与祝英台》是越剧的代表作。它们都是代表中华民族优秀传统文化的经典之作。

A: 中国传统文化博大精深，令人叹为观止，听了你的讲解，我都迫不及待想欣赏了。

B: 河南电视台播出了一个名叫《梨园春》的综艺节目，如果你想欣赏更多中国传统戏曲，这对你来说是一个更好的选择。

生词注解　Notes

① popularity /ˌpɒpjuˈlærətɪ/　*n.* 人气；流行

② acclaim /əˈkleɪm/　*vt.* 称赞；高度评价

③ prominent /ˈprɒmɪnənt/　*adj.* 著名的；杰出的

④ batch /bætʃ/　*n.* 一批；批次

⑤ sonorous /ˈsɒnərəs/　*adj.* 铿锵的；雄浑的

⑥ cadence /ˈkeɪdns/　*n.* 抑扬顿挫；韵律

⑦ demonstrate /ˈdemənstreɪt/　*vt.* 显示；表现

⑧ respectively /rɪˈspektɪvlɪ/　*adv.* 分别地；各自地

编钟

Chime Bells

 导入语　Lead-in

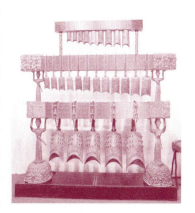

编钟是中国古代一种重要的打击乐器，源于夏朝，盛于春秋战国直至秦汉。中国是最早制造和使用编钟的国家。编钟在中国古代是上层社会专用的乐器，是等级和权力的象征，多用于宫廷演奏，主要用于国家征战、朝见或祭祀等活动，较少流传于民间。编钟由青铜铸成，由若干个大小不同的钟按照音调高低的次序排列，悬挂在钟架上，用小木槌按照乐谱敲打铜钟，可以演奏出美妙的乐曲。编钟在不同时期具有不同的形状和图案，如1978年发掘的战国曾侯乙编钟，钟上刻有人、兽、龙、花等图形和标有许多与乐律有关的音乐术语，是我国迄今发现数量最多、保存最完好、音律最全的一套编钟。

文化剪影 Cultural Outline

Chime bells, originated in the Xia Dynasty and was cast from bronze, was an important ancient Chinese musical instrument. In addition to being used for court performances, such as signaling to participate in the war, announce major events, offer sacrifices to ancestors, entertain, mourn and so on, the chime bells were also regarded as **patriotic**① symbols and war **trophies**②.

编钟源于夏朝,由青铜铸成,是中国古代的一种重要乐器。除了用于宫廷表演,如宣战、宣布重大事件、祭祀祖先、娱乐和悼念等活动外,编钟也被视为爱国的象征和战利品。

Chime bells of Marquis Yi of Zeng, engraved with human, animal, dragon, flower and other patterns, as well as music scores, was the most well-preserved, the largest in number, the most complete type of chime, fully demonstrating the advanced level of ancient Chinese music culture.

曾侯乙编钟上刻有人、兽、龙、花等图案,且标有乐谱,是目前保存最完好、数量最多、音律最全的编钟,充分展示了中国古代音乐文化的先进水平。

Chime bells widely **distributed**③ geographically, is said to possess special magical powers such as **inducing**④ rain, **dispelling**⑤ wind, warding off evil spirits and removing curses, with a certain cultural status and unique cultural **connotation**⑥.

编钟在地理上分布广泛,据说其具有召雨、驱风、辟邪和除咒等特殊魔力,也具有一定的文化地位和独特的文化内涵。

佳句点睛　Punchlines

1. Chime bells mainly adopted in the court performances was a vital musical instrument in ancient China.

编钟主要用于宫廷演出,是中国古代的一件重要乐器。

2. Chime bells fully showcased the unique charm of ancient Chinese music culture, one typical representative of which was chime bells of Marquis Yi of Zeng.

编钟充分展示了中国古代音乐文化的独特魅力,其中一个典型代表就是曾侯乙编钟。

3. Chime bells enjoyed the unique cultural connotation and **irreplaceable**⑦ cultural status.

编钟具有独特的文化内涵和不可替代的文化地位。

生词注解　Notes

① patriotic /ˌpætriˈɒtɪk/　*adj.* 爱国的

② trophy /ˈtrəʊfi/　*n.* 战利品;奖品

③ distribute /dɪˈstrɪbjuːt/　*vt.* 分配；分发

④ induce /ɪnˈdjuːs/　*vt.* 诱使；引起

⑤ dispel /dɪˈspel/　*vt.* 驱散；消除

⑥ connotation /ˌkɒnəˈteɪʃn/　*n.* 内涵；含蓄

⑦ irreplaceable /ˌɪrɪˈpleɪsəbl/　*adj.* (因贵重或独特)不能替代的；独一无二的

古琴

Guqin

 导入语 Lead-in

古琴,也称"瑶琴""玉琴"或"七弦琴"等,是中国传统的拨弦乐器。早在周朝时期,除了用于国家祭祀、朝会和典礼等活动以外,古琴也兴盛于民间,是一件非常普遍和受人喜爱的乐器。齐桓公的"号钟"、楚庄王的"绕梁"、司马相如的"绿绮"和蔡邕的"焦尾"被人们誉为"四大名琴"。古琴代表曲目有《广陵散》《高山流水》等。古琴因其优美的造型和音色以及清、和、淡、雅的音乐风格而备受青睐,"高山流水""琴瑟和鸣""弦外之音""对牛弹琴"等成语都蕴含了丰厚的琴文化元素。2003年,联合国教科文组织将中国古琴列入"第二批人类口头与非物质遗产"。2006年,古琴被国务院列入《第一批国家级非物质文化遗产名录》。

 文化剪影 Cultural Outline

Guqin, also known as the "seven-stringed instrument", is a traditional Chinese **plucked**① string instrument with a history of more than four thousand years. As a representative musical instrument of Chinese traditional music culture, guqin enjoyed great popularity in the ancient times.

古琴,又称"七弦琴",是中国传统的弹拨弦乐器,已有四千多年的历史。作为中国传统音乐文化的代表乐器,古琴在古代广受欢迎。

Guqin can be plucked out beautiful sounds and make people feel peace, **tranquility**②, lightness and even the harmony of nature. It embodies the peak of moral **cultivation**③ before ancient chess, **calligraphy**④ and painting, **favored**⑤ by ancient **literati**⑥, with the **representative**⑦ work *High Mountains and Flowing Water*.

古琴能弹拨出动听的声音,并使人体会到平和、宁静、轻盈甚至大自然的和谐,体现了古代棋、书、画之前道德修养的顶峰,受到了古代文人的青睐,代表曲目有《高山流水》。

Guqin's beautiful melody helps people to **maintain**⑧ inner peace and balance, and is used as a personal emotional comfort. In addition, the seven-stringed instrument is also regarded as a necessary condition for the development of ancient civilizations, reflecting the traditional cultural values of **clarity**[9], delicacy and simplicity.

古琴优美的旋律有助于人们保持内心的平静和平衡，被用作个人情感的慰藉。此外，七弦琴还被尊为古代文明发展的必备条件，体现了清澈、细腻和简朴的传统文化价值。

佳句点睛 Punchlines

1. As a traditional Chinese plucked string instrument, guqin is time-honored and well-received musical instrument in ancient times.

古琴是中国传统的弹拨弦乐器，在古代是久负盛名的乐器。

2. Guqin, together with game of go, calligraphy and painting are top four on the list of moral cultivation for the literati in ancient times.

古琴与围棋、书、画并列为古代文人道德修养的前四名。

3. Guqin showcases the traditional cultural values of purity, delicacy and simplicity through its wonderful and harmonious melodies.

古琴以其美妙和谐的旋律展示了纯洁、细腻和朴素的传统文化价值。

生词注解 Notes

① pluck /plʌk/　*vt.* 弹拨；摘
② tranquility /træŋˈkwɪlətɪ/　*n.* 宁静；安宁

民 俗 文 化

③ cultivation /ˌkʌltɪˈveɪʃn/ n. 培养；培育

④ calligraphy /kəˈlɪɡrəfɪ/ n. 书法；书法艺术

⑤ favor /ˈfeɪvə(r)/ vt. 宠爱；偏爱

⑥ literati /ˌlɪtəˈrɑːtɪ/ n. 学士；文人

⑦ representative /ˌreprɪˈzentətɪv/ adj. 典型的；有代表性的

⑧ maintain /meɪnˈteɪn/ vt. 维持；主张

⑨ clarity /ˈklærətɪ/ n. 清楚；明晰

古筝

Guzheng

导入语　Lead-in

战国时期，古筝兴盛于秦地，故又名"秦筝"，也称"汉筝"或"瑶筝"等，是中国传统民族乐器之一，属于弹拨弦乐器，被称为"万乐之祖，众乐之尊"和"中国第一国乐"。古筝外形古朴典雅，美观大方。古筝的音质关键取决于面板和琴弦，面板材质主要为桐木，琴弦按五音定弦，不同时期和地区有不同的定弦法，目前古筝规格统一定为二十一根弦。古筝音色优美圆润，发音清脆悦耳，极具民族特色和感染力，是第一件走向世界的中国民族乐器。演奏古筝不仅能让人修身怡情、培养高洁气质，而且是弘扬中国优秀传统文化的重要媒介。古筝名曲有《渔舟唱晚》《出水莲》《高山流水》《林冲夜奔》《侗族舞曲》《汉宫秋月》等。

文化剪影　Cultural Outline

Guzheng (Chinese **zither**①), which now has twenty-one strings, is a traditional Chinese plucked string instrument that dates back two thousand five hundred years. It was popular among people from all walks of life in ancient China, showcasing a distinct and rich traditional Chinese music culture.

古筝目前有二十一根弦，是一种中国传统的拨弦乐器，距今已有两千五百年的历史。古筝在古代各阶层人士中广受欢迎，能够展现鲜明而丰富的中国传统音乐文化。

When playing the guzheng, performers often wear finger picks, which are made of different materials such as ivory, turtle shell, shell, **resin**② or hard plastic, on the right hand or on both hands. In addition, if played in **designated**③ ways, it would often produce sounds of waterfalls, thunder, and even music with beautiful country scenes, its well-known representative masterpieces being *Songs of Fishing Boat at Dusk*, *High Mountains and Flowing Water*, and so on.

演奏古筝时，表演者通常右手或双手佩戴由象牙、龟壳、贝壳、树脂或硬塑料等不同材料制成的义甲。此外，如果按照特定的方式演奏，古筝往往会发出瀑布声、雷声，甚至能呈现出描绘优美乡村画面的音乐，古筝名曲有《渔舟唱晚》《高山流水》等。

In solo, **trio**[④], accompaniment and instrumental **ensemble**[⑤], the performance of the guzheng requires a series of skills to produce clear, slender, profound, lively, beautiful and **gorgeous**[⑥] tones, which can achieve the effect of peace of mind and **exotic**[⑦] artistic conception.

在独奏、三重奏、伴奏和器乐合奏中,需要一系列演奏技巧,才能使古筝发出清脆、纤细、深邃、明快、优美、华丽的音韵,达到让人心境宁静和展现奇异意境的效果。

佳句点睛 Punchlines

1. Guzheng has a long history, reflecting the bright and rich traditional Chinese music culture.

古筝历史悠久,体现了鲜明而丰富的中国传统音乐文化。

2. Guzheng can produce vivid sounds true to life, displaying the **authentic**[⑧] and original features of Chinese musical instruments.

古筝能发出生动逼真的声音,表现出中国乐器原汁原味的特点。

3. Guzheng helps people to get a peaceful mood and a wonderful feeling.

古筝有助于人们获得宁静的心情和美妙的感受。

民俗文化

情景对话 Situational Dialogue

A: Hi, welcome to our musical instrument shop. Which kind of instrument do you wanna buy?

B: Hi, I just wanna look around and learn about some traditional Chinese musical instruments, buy one that is easy to learn. Can you give me some suggestions?

A: Yes, I can. Traditional Chinese musical instruments are the wisdom of the working people in ancient China. According to the different characteristics of performance methods, they are divided into four categories: wind instruments, such as xiao, sheng, bamboo flute, and so on; stringed instruments, such as erhu, gaohu, banhu, and so on; plucked string instruments, such as guzheng, pipa, guqin, and so on; **percussion**⑧ instruments: chime bells, gongs and drums, and so on.

B: Very good. Which kind instrument is easy to learn?

A: Frankly speaking, guzheng is a traditional plucked string musical instrument popular in the folk, with a **distinctive**⑨ and rich characteristic of Chinese traditional music culture.

B: After hearing your introduction, I wanna learn to play the guzheng, which is a typical traditional Chinese musical instrument.

A: 嗨,欢迎光临我们的乐器店,你想买哪种乐器?

B: 嗨,我想四处看看了解一些中国传统乐器,买一件容易学的,你能给我一些建议吗?

A: 能。中国传统乐器是中国古代劳动人民的智慧。根据演奏方法的不同特点,将其分为四类:吹管乐器,如箫、笙、竹笛等;拉弦乐器,如二胡、高胡、板胡等;弹拨弦乐,如古筝、琵琶、古琴等;打击乐器,如编钟、锣鼓等。

B: 很好。哪种乐器好学啊?

A: 坦率地说,古筝是一种流行于民间的传统拨弦乐器,具有鲜明而丰富的中国传统音乐文化特征。

B: 听了你的介绍,我想学习古筝,这是一种典型的中国传统乐器。

生词注解 Notes

① zither /ˈzɪðə(r)/ n. 筝;齐特琴

② resin /ˈrezɪn/ n. 树脂;合成树脂

③ designated /ˈdezɪɡneɪtɪd/ adj. 指定的;特指的

④ trio /ˈtriːəʊ/ n. 三重奏;三重唱

⑤ ensemble /ɒnˈsɒmbl/ n. 合奏;舞剧团(全体人员)

⑥ gorgeous /ˈɡɔːdʒəs/ adj. 华丽的;灿烂的

⑦ exotic /ɪɡˈzɒtɪk/ adj. 异国情调的;外来的

⑧ authentic /ɔːˈθentɪk/ adj. 真正的;真实的

琵琶

Pipa

 导入语　Lead-in

琵琶最早出现在秦朝,是一种历史悠久的中国弹拨乐器,被称为"弹拨乐器之王"和"弹拨乐器首座"等。"琵""琶"是根据演奏弹拨乐器时的右手技法而命名的。"琵"和"琶"原是两种弹奏手法,"琵"是右手向前弹,"琶"是右手向后挑。琵琶的寓意为"二玉相碰",发出悦耳的碰击声。琵琶一般是木制或竹制,颈与面板上设有确定音位的"相"和"品"。

经过历代演奏者的改良,目前琵琶的统一规格为六相二十四品的四弦琵琶。弹奏时,表演者通常竖抱琵琶,左手按弦,右手戴赛璐珞或玳瑁等材料制成的假指甲拨弦弹奏。琵琶音域宽广,声音穿透力强,表现力丰富,是弘扬和传播中华优秀传统文化的重要民族乐器,代表曲目有《十面埋伏》《塞上曲》等。

文化剪影　Cultural Outline

　　Pipa is a plucked string instrument. It is said that it was introduced from western Asia to the hinterland in the late Eastern Han Dynasty, and gradually **evolved**① into a **multifunctional**② musical instrument suitable for solo, ensemble and **accompaniment**③.

　　琵琶是一种弹拨乐器。据说它是东汉末年从西亚地区传入内地，逐步演变成适合独奏、合奏与伴奏的一种多功能乐器。

　　Pipa is honored as "The King of Plucked Instruments" and "The First Plucked Instrument", well-known for its strong **penetrating**④ sounds and rich expressiveness. And what's more, it is an important national instrument to carry forward and spread the excellent traditional Chinese culture.

　　琵琶被誉为"弹拨乐器之王"和"弹拨乐器首座"，以强烈的穿透力和丰富的表现力而著称。更重要的是，琵琶是弘扬和传播中国优秀传统文化的重要民族乐器。

　　Pipa is usually made of wood or bamboo, has four strings on the neck and face plate and is tuned by "xiang" and "pin". During the performance, the performer generally would hold it upright, press the strings with the left hand and play with the strings of false nails made of **celluloid**⑤ or tortoiseshell with the right hand, and make a beautiful, fine, passionate, heroic sound.

　　琵琶通常由木头或竹子制成，颈部和面板上有四根弦，由"相"和

"品"来定音。演奏时,演奏者将琵琶竖起,左手按弦,右手用赛璐珞或玳瑁制成的护甲弹奏,发出优美细腻、激昂豪迈的声音。

佳句点睛　Punchlines

1. Pipa is a **versatile**⑥ instrument, which is used for solo, ensembles and accompaniment.

琵琶是一种多功能乐器,用于独奏、合奏和伴奏。

2. Pipa is an important national instrument to carry forward the brilliant traditional Chinese culture.

琵琶是弘扬中华优秀传统文化的重要民族乐器。

3. Pipa can make a beautiful, fine, passionate, heroic sound, which is **exhilarating**⑦.

琵琶能发出优美细腻、激昂豪迈的声音,使人欢欣鼓舞。

生词注解　Notes

① evolve /ɪˈvɒlv/　*vi.* 进化;逐步形成

② multifunctional /ˌmʌltɪˈfʌŋkʃənl/　*adj.* 多功能的

③ accompaniment /əˈkʌmpənɪmənt/　*n.* 伴奏;伴随物

④ penetrating /ˈpenətreɪtɪŋ/　*adj.* 穿透力的;锐利的

⑤ celluloid /ˈseljulɔɪd/　*n.* 赛璐珞;(旧时摄影用的)胶片

⑥ versatile /ˈvɜːsətaɪl/　*adj.* 通用的;万能的

⑦ exhilarating /ɪɡˈzɪləreɪtɪŋ/　*adj.* 令人欢欣的;令人振奋的

二胡

Erhu

 导入语 Lead-in

二胡,始于唐朝,是中国传统拉弦乐器。二胡最早源于中国古代北方少数民族,当时被称为"奚琴"。唐朝时,西方和北方各民族被称为"胡人",他们的乐器统称为"胡琴"。二胡一般按产地或琴筒构造分类,按产地分为江西琴、北京琴、苏州琴等,按琴筒构造分为圆筒二胡、八角二胡、六角二胡等。琴筒是二胡的重要组成部分,一般由檀木或红木制作而成。二胡的弹奏原理是通过弓在琴筒上的推拉运动而产生发音共鸣体,因此琴筒的质地和形状对二胡的音质具有直接影响。二胡的表演内容丰富,表现力强,既能呈现出悲痛凄惨的情景,也能展现出气势恢宏的意境,代表曲目《二泉映月》彰显了中国传统乐器的独特魅力。

文化剪影 Cultural Outline

Erhu, known as "huqin" or "xiqin" is a traditional Chinese two-stringed instrument, dating back to over one thousand years ago. The people of western and northern China in the Tang Dynasty were known as the Hu people, and their instruments were known as huqin, hence erhu, which originated from the **ethnic**[①] minorities of northern China, was also called huqin.

二胡,又称"胡琴"或"奚琴",是中国传统的两弦乐器,可以追溯到一千多年前。唐朝时,西方和北方各民族被称为"胡人",他们的乐器被称为"胡琴",因此源于中国北方少数民族的二胡也被称为"胡琴"。

The performance of erhu is rich in content and **expressive**[②]. It can not only play sad but stirring tunes, but also show a magnificent, high-spirited mood. The representative work *The Two Springs Reflecting the Moon* embodies the unique charm of traditional Chinese instruments.

二胡的表演内容丰富,表现力强,既能弹奏出悲壮的曲调,又能呈现出波澜壮阔、昂扬向上的意境,代表曲目《二泉映月》彰显了中国传统乐器的独特魅力。

Like an upside-down two-string hammer, erhu is known as the

"Chinese violin" or the "Chinese two-string violin". Mainly made of sandalwood or **mahogany**③, it produces a sonorous mid-treble sound that can be used as a solo instrument, as well as in small ensembles and large **orchestras**④, expressing strong emotions with its **penetrating**⑤ sound.

二胡就像一把上下颠倒的两弦锤子,被称为"中国小提琴"或"中国二弦小提琴"。二胡主要由檀香木或红木制成,演奏时产生中高音为主的洪亮声音,既可作为独奏乐器,也可用于小型合奏和大型管弦乐队演奏,通过穿透性的声音表达强烈的情感。

佳句点睛 Punchlines

1. Erhu is a traditional Chinese two-stringed instrument, which originated from the ethnic minority in the north of ancient China
二胡是中国传统的二弦乐器,源于中国古代北方的少数民族。

2. Erhu is a versatile instrument embodying the unique charm of traditional Chinese musical instruments.
二胡是一种多功能乐器,体现了中国传统乐器的独特魅力。

3. Erhu, which expresses strong emotions through its penetrating sound, is considered one of the popular instrument.
二胡通过穿透性的声音来表达强烈的情感,被视为广受欢迎的乐器之一。

 生词注解 Notes

① ethnic /ˈeθnɪk/ *adj.* 种族的；人种的

② expressive /ɪkˈspresɪv/ *adj.* 富于表现力的

③ mahogany /məˈhɒgənɪ/ *n.* 红木；桃花心木

④ orchestra /ˈɔːkɪstrə/ *n.* 管弦乐队

⑤ penetrating /ˈpenətreɪtɪŋ/ *adj.* 穿透的；尖锐的

箫

Xiao

导入语 Lead-in

箫，又称"排箫"或"洞箫"，是中国古老的吹奏乐器之一，可追溯到远古时代。箫一般由竹子制成，也有玉箫和铜箫等。箫为单管，竖吹，共六个音孔，吹孔和音孔必须在一条直线上，上端为吹孔，中间和下方位置为音孔。箫的演奏主要与呼吸技法、演奏姿势和手指技法密切相关。箫的音色空灵自然、轻柔典雅，富有大自然的灵性和淡雅，适合独奏和重奏。表演者在演奏时，需要保持一种平和、安宁的心境，才能吹奏出空灵穿透的美妙声音。另外，箫也是古时文人颇为喜爱的乐器，如唐朝诗人杜牧曾有"二十四桥明月夜，玉人何处教吹箫"等诗句。

民俗文化

文化剪影 Cultural Outline

Xiao is a kind of **vertical**① bamboo flute with a long history. It is usually divided into the single-tube jade flute and the bronze flute. There are six sound holes, which can produce soft and beautiful sound suitable for solo and ensemble.

箫是一种历史悠久的竖吹竹笛，通常分为单管玉箫和铜箫，共有六个音孔，发出适合独奏和合奏的柔和优美的声音。

Xiao is a traditional wind instrument in China. Its performance is closely related to breathing skills, playing **posture**②, fingering, and so on. Players need to maintain a peaceful mood when playing, in order to make this wonderful sound of **ethereal**③ penetration.

箫是中国传统的风琴，它的演奏与呼吸技巧、演奏姿势、手指技法等密切相关，演奏者在演奏时需要保持一种平和的心境，才能吹奏出空灵穿透的美妙声音。

Xiao is ethereal and natural, gentle and elegant, honored as an instrument filled with spiritual nature and light elegance. It has generally been viewed as something in common with the thought of inaction **advocated**④ by Taoism, so it was favored by ancient scholars.

箫的音色空灵自然，轻柔典雅，被誉为一种充满自然灵性和淡雅的乐器。它与道教倡导的无为思想有着共同之处，因而受到古代学者的青睐。

佳句点睛 Punchlines

1. Xiao is a vertical flute bamboo flute with a soft and beautiful tone, suitable for solo and ensemble.

箫是一种竖吹竹笛,音色柔和优美,适合独奏和合奏。

2. Xiao is a traditional Chinese orchestral instrument, and the player can only play this penetrating ethereal sound with a peaceful mind.

箫是一种中国传统的管弦乐器,演奏者只有保持平和的心境才能吹奏出这种具有穿透力的空灵声音。

3. The sound of xiao is imbued with **spirituality**⑤ and elegance, echoing the thought of Taoism non-interference.

箫声透着灵性与淡雅,与道家的无为思想相呼应。

生词注解 Notes

① vertical /ˈvɜːtɪkl/ *adj.* 垂直的;竖的

② posture /ˈpɒstʃə(r)/ *n.* 姿势;态度

③ ethereal /ɪˈθɪəriəl/ *adj.* 空灵的;轻飘的

④ advocate /ˈædvəkət/ *vt.* 提倡;倡导

⑤ spirituality /ˌspɪrɪtʃuˈælətɪ/ *n.* 灵性;精神性

锣鼓

Gongs and Drums

导入语　Lead-in

锣鼓是一种声响强烈、节奏鲜明的中国民俗乐器，始于尧舜时期。锣鼓的伴奏不仅可以增强中国戏曲表演的节奏感和动作的准确性，还有助于表现人物情绪，渲染和烘托舞台气氛。戏曲锣鼓分为锣、钹和鼓。每种乐器根据形状、制作和用途的不同，又有各自丰富的品种及名称，如锣钹类有铮锣、大锣、小锣、大钹、小钹和铰子等。演奏锣鼓时，要根据需要有组织、有规律地编排各种乐器，并按照鼓板指挥击奏出有节奏、有规律的音响。最著名的锣鼓为山西一带的威风锣鼓，它节奏明快、气势恢宏，让人感到威武霸气，不仅能传达出劳动人民勤劳勇敢、善良朴实的个性，也能展示出中华儿女奋发图强、英勇顽强的民族气魄，享有"华夏第一鼓"的美誉。2006年，晋南威风锣鼓被国务院列入《第一批国家级非物质文化遗产名录》。

文化剪影　Cultural Outline

Gongs and drums that **originated**① from the period of Yao and Shun are a kind of Chinese folk musical instrument with a history of more than four thousand years. They have a strong sound and a clear rhythm while their **accompaniment**② helps to improve the rhythm and **accuracy**③ of the performance of the opera, express the emotions of the characters, and **render**④ or set off the stage atmosphere.

锣鼓源于尧舜时期,是一种具有四千多年历史的中国民间乐器。锣鼓具有强烈的声音和鲜明的节奏,其伴奏有助于提高戏曲表演的节奏性和准确性,抒发人物的情感,渲染和衬托舞台气氛。

The most famous are Majestic Gongs and Drums in Shanxi, with a bright rhythm and magnificent **momentum**⑤, which make people feel awe-inspiring, show the national spirit of the brave and **tenacious**⑥ Chinese people, and enjoy the fame of "The First Drum in China".

最著名的锣鼓为山西一带的威风锣鼓,它节奏明快、气势恢宏,让人感到威武霸气,展示了中华儿女勇敢顽强的民族气魄,享有"华夏第一鼓"的美誉。

Gongs and drums in the Chinese opera are generally divided into gongs, **cymbals**⑦ and drums. When beating gongs and drums, the performer should arrange various musical instruments according to the

needs, make rhythmic and regular sounds according to the direction of the drum board, and display the hardworking, brave spirit of the working people as well as the kind and simple personality.

中国戏曲中的锣鼓一般分为锣、钹和鼓,演奏锣鼓时,演奏者应根据需要摆放各种乐器,并按鼓板的方向演奏出有节奏、有规律的声音,表现出劳动人民勤劳勇敢的精神和善良朴实的个性。

佳句点睛 Punchlines

1. The gongs and drums have a strong voice and a bright rhythm, which helps to express the emotions of the characters and render or set off the stage atmosphere.

锣鼓声音强烈,节奏鲜明,有助于抒发人物情感,渲染或烘托舞台气氛。

2. The Majestic Gongs and Drums have a bright rhythm and great momentum, which makes people feel awe-inspiring, reflecting the national spirit of the Chinese people.

威风锣鼓节奏明快、气势恢宏,让人感到威武霸气,体现了中国人民的民族气魄。

3. Gongs and drums display the hard-working, brave, kind and simple personality of the Chinese people.

锣鼓展示了中国人民勤劳、勇敢、善良、朴素的个性。

生词注解 Notes

① originate /əˈrɪdʒɪneɪt/ *vi.* 发源;起源

② accompaniment /əˈkʌmpənɪmənt/ *n.* 伴奏;伴随物

③ accuracy /ˈækjərəsɪ/ *n.* 精确度;准确性

④ render /ˈrendə/ *vt.* 渲染;表演

⑤ momentum /məˈmentəm/ *n.* 势头;动量

⑥ tenacious /təˈneɪʃəs/ *adj.* 顽强的;坚韧的

⑦ cymbal /ˈsɪmbl/ *n.* 钹;铙钹

第二部分 书画与手工艺

Part II Calligraphy, Painting and Handicrafts

书法

Calligraphy

 导入语　Lead-in

书法是中国汉字在发展过程中产生的一种独特的传统艺术，是指借助文房四宝抒发情感的一门艺术，因此书法的产生和毛笔的发明密切相关。书法艺术以汉字为载体，早期作品为象形文字或图画文字。中国书法的发展包括古代书法和现代书法两个时期。古代书法包括甲骨文、金文和篆书，现代书法包括隶书、楷书、草书和行书。中国书法通过简练的线条造型，表现出含蓄复杂的意境和情趣，散发着独特的艺术魅力。只有从笔法、字法、构法、章法、墨法和笔势等方面进行鉴赏和品味，才能真正感受和领悟到中国书法艺术的博大精深和源远流长。

文化剪影 Cultural Outline

Chinese calligraphy originated in the development of Chinese characters, and its early works were **hieroglyphs**① or **pictographs**②. The birth of calligraphy was closely related to the invention of the four treasures of the study, especially that of brush, by virtue of which the beauty and **connotation**③ of calligraphy art is naturally and smoothly expressed.

中国书法产生于汉字的发展过程中，早期作品为象形文字或图画文字。书法的诞生与文房四宝尤其是毛笔的发明密不可分，文房四宝使书法艺术的美与内涵得以自然流畅的表达。

The development of Chinese calligraphy has experienced two stages: ancient calligraphy and modern calligraphy. The former includes **oracle**④ bone **inscriptions**⑤, bronze inscriptions and seal script while the latter consist of official script, regular script, **cursive**⑥ script and running script.

中国书法的发展经历了古代书法和现代书法两个阶段。前者包括甲骨文、金文和篆书，后者包括隶书、楷书、草书和行书。

Chinese calligraphy shows a subtle, complex artistic conception through simple line modeling, which **radiates**⑦ a unique artistic charm. The appreciation of Chinese calligraphy art can be realized from the aspects of calligraphy, characters, lines, composition, pen and ink, style, and so on.

中国书法通过简单的线条造型表现出含蓄复杂的意境，散发出独特的艺术魅力。中国书法艺术可以从书法、文字、线条、构图、笔墨和风格等方面进行欣赏和品味。

佳句点睛 Punchlines

1. Chinese calligraphy was closely related to the invention of the four treasures of the study, especially that of brush.

中国书法与文房四宝尤其是毛笔的发明关系密切。

2. The development of Chinese calligraphy has experienced two stages: ancient calligraphy and modern calligraphy.

中国书法的发展经历了古代书法和现代书法两个阶段。

3. Chinese calligraphy shows a subtle, complex artistic conception through simple line modeling, which radiates a unique artistic charm.

中国书法以简单的线条造型表现出含蓄复杂的意境，散发出独特的艺术魅力。

情景对话 Situational Dialogue

A: I saw you posted some great pictures in your circle of friends. Where were you last weekend?

B: Oh, I went to the Yin Ruins Museum, which was the site of an ancient capital city 3,000 years ago. The pictures are about the oracle bone inscriptions, one form of Chinese calligraphy.

A: What else do you know about Chinese calligraphy?

B: It is divided into ancient calligraphy and modern calligraphy. The former includes oracle bone inscriptions, bronze inscriptions and seal script while the latter consists of official script, regular script, cursive script and running script. In addition, Chinese calligraphy shows its **implicit**[⑧] and complex artistic conception through its simple line modeling.

A: After hearing your introduction, I have had a general knowledge of Chinese calligraphy.

B: Alright. There are also many well-known calligraphers, for example, Chairman Mao of the People's Republic of China, was an expert of cursive script.

A: That's great. So brilliant is the Chinese calligraphy that I cannot wait to appreciate its works of art.

B: OK. You'd better go to the gallery in our city, where you can appreciate more.

A: 我看到你在朋友圈里发布了一些很不错的照片。上周末你去哪儿了？

B: 噢，我去了殷墟博物馆，那是三千年前的一座古城遗址。这些图片是甲骨文，甲骨文是中国书法的一种形式。

A: 你对中国书法还有哪些了解？

B: 中国书法分为古代书法和现代书法。前者包括甲骨文、金文和篆书，后者包括隶书、楷书、草书和行书。另外，中国书法通过简单的线条造型表现出含蓄复杂的意境。

A: 听了你的介绍，我对中国书法有了一定的了解。

B: 很好，中国还有很多著名的书法家，比如中华人民共和国的毛主席就是一位草书书法家。

A: 太精彩了，我都迫不及待地想欣赏中国书法艺术作品了。

B: 好的，你可以去我们城市的艺术馆，在那里你可以欣赏到更多的书法艺术作品。

生词注解 Notes

① hieroglyph /ˈhaɪərəglɪf/　*n.* 象形文字

② pictograph /ˈpɪktəgrɑːf/　*n.* 图画文字

③ connotation /ˌkɒnəˈteɪʃn/　*n.* 内涵；含义

④ oracle /ˈɒrəkl/　*n.* 甲骨文；神谕

⑤ inscription /ɪnˈskrɪpʃn/　*n.* 铭刻；题词

⑥ cursive /ˈkɜːsɪv/　*adj.* 草书的；草书体的

⑦ radiate /ˈreɪdieɪt/　*vt.* 流露；表现

⑧ implicit /ɪmˈplɪsɪt/　*adj.* 含蓄的；内涵的

中国画

Traditional Chinese Painting

导入语　Lead-in

中国画,古称"丹青",源于汉代。中国画在世界画坛上是唯一以国家名称命名的画,它体现了民族艺术和民族审美心理的创新与发展,在世界美术领域中独树一帜,自成体系。中国画主要指用毛笔、墨、国画颜料等在宣纸、绢、帛上作画并加以装裱的卷轴画。中国画按题材分为人物画、山水画和花鸟画,按技法分为工笔画和写意画。中国画是用艺术表现的一种观念和思想,体现了古人对自然、社会以及与之关联的政治、哲学、宗教、道德和文艺等的认知。因此,只有从中国画的气韵、意境、笔墨、画法、留白,以及诗、书、画、篆刻等方面进行鉴赏,才能领略中国绘画艺术的意境和精髓。中国画的代表画家有关山月、张大千等。

文化剪影 Cultural Outline

Traditional Chinese painting, known as "danqing" in ancient times, originated in the Han Dynasty. Chinese painting embodies the innovation and development of national art and **aesthetic**① psychology, forming its own system and unique schools.

中国画，古称"丹青"，源于汉代。中国画体现了民族艺术和民族审美心理的创新与发展，形成了自己的体系和独特的流派。

Chinese painting mainly refers to **scroll**② paintings on the rice paper and silk painted with brush, ink and traditional Chinese painting **pigment**③, which are **mounted**④ and framed. Chinese painting can be divided into figure painting, landscape painting and flower-and-bird painting. Ink-and-wash painting is the representative of Chinese painting.

中国画主要是指在宣纸和丝绸上用毛笔、水墨和国画颜料等在宣纸和丝绸上作画并加以装裱的卷轴画。中国画按题材可分为人物画、山水画和花鸟画。水墨画是中国画的代表。

The concept and thought of Chinese painting vividly expressed the ancient people's understanding of nature, society, politics, philosophy, religion, **morality**⑤, literature and art through painting art. Therefore, only through the artistic conception of Chinese painting, ink, painting, blank as well as poetry, painting and seal carving appreciation, can we truly understand the artistic conception and **essence**⑥ of Chinese painting.

中国画的观念和思想通过绘画艺术生动传达出古人对自然、社会、政治、哲学、宗教、道德、文学艺术等的认识。因此，只有通过对中国画的意境、笔墨、画法、留白，以及诗、书、画篆刻等进行鉴赏，才能真正了解中国画的意境和精髓。

 佳句点睛　Punchlines

1. Chinese painting embodies the innovation and development of national art and the aesthetic mind of the nation.

中国画体现了民族艺术和民族审美心理的创新与发展。

2. Chinese painting mainly refers to scroll paintings painted on the rice paper and silk which are mounted and framed.

中国画主要是指装裱在宣纸和丝绸上的卷轴画。

3. Chinese painting embodies the ancient people's understanding of nature, society, politics, philosophy, religion, morality, literature and art, and so on.

中国画体现了古人对自然、社会、政治、哲学、宗教、道德和文学艺术等的认识。

情景对话 Situational Dialogue

A: Hi.

B: Hi. I've heard your art exhibition is to be held next week. Can you share your views about Chinese paintings here?

A: Sure. Traditional Chinese painting refers to scroll paintings on rice paper and silk painted with brush, ink and traditional Chinese painting pigment, which are mounted and framed.

B: Oh, amazing, can you talk about more about its classification?

A: Yes, I can. According to the theme, Chinese painting can be divided into figure, landscape, and flower and bird. Ink-and-wash painting is the representative of Chinese painting.

B: Oh, well said. Does your art exhibition contain all the themes of Chinese painting?

A: Sure. When appreciating Chinese painting, we advise you **appreciate**① them in terms of its artistic conception, ink, painting method, poetry, painting and seal so that you can have a knowledge of its artistic conception and essence.

B: Alright. Thank you very much. Wish everything goes well with your art exhibition.

A: 你好。

B: 你好。听说你的艺术展将于下周举行。你能分享一下对中

国画的看法吗?

A: 当然能,中国画是指用毛笔、墨水和国画颜料等在宣纸和丝绸上作画并加以装裱的卷轴画。

B: 噢,太棒了,你能多谈谈它的种类吗?

A: 好的。中国画按题材可分为人物画、山水画和花鸟画。水墨画是中国画的代表。

B: 噢,说得好。你的艺术展包含了中国画的所有主题吗?

A: 当然,在欣赏中国画的时候,可以从中国画的意境、水墨、画法,以及诗、书、画、篆刻等方面来欣赏,这样才能了解中国画的意境和本质。

B: 好的,多谢。祝你的艺术展一切顺利。

生词注解　Notes

① aesthetic /iːsˈθetɪk/　*adj.* 审美的;美学的

② scroll /skrəʊl/　*n.* 卷轴;条幅

③ pigment /ˈpɪgmənt/　*n.* 颜料;色素

④ mount /ˈmaʊnt/　*vt.* 装裱;安装

⑤ morality /məˈrælətɪ/　*n.* 道德;品行

⑥ essence /ˈesns/　*n.* 精华;本质

⑦ appreciate /əˈpriːʃɪeɪt/　*vt.* 欣赏;理解

篆刻

Seal Cutting

导入语 Lead-in

篆刻艺术源于先秦时代，主要是书法和镌刻结合在一起，用来制作印章。篆刻广义上称为"雕镂铭刻"，狭义上称为"治印之学"，治印之学也被直接称为"刻印""铁笔""铁书"和"刻图章"等。印章刻制的材料有铜、石、金、玉、木、牙、骨、砖和有机玻璃制品等，但篆刻艺术用材主要以石质材料为主。篆刻艺术是一门与书法密切结合的艺术形式，用刻刀在石头上写书法。篆刻书法主要采用甲骨文、金文、战国文、大篆和小篆等。2009年，中国篆刻被联合国教科文组织列入《人类非物质文化遗产代表作名录》。

文化剪影　Cultural Outline

The art of seal cutting originated from the pre-Qin period. As a unique art form of Chinese characters, the art of seal cutting mainly refers to the combination of calligraphy and carving, with a series of names in ancient times, **symbolizing**① power and status.

篆刻艺术源于先秦时期。作为一门独特的汉字艺术形式,篆刻艺术主要是指书法与雕刻相结合的艺术,在古代有一系列名称,象征着权力和地位。

Seal cutting is a unique art form, combining calligraphy, rules and knife techniques perfectly. In 2009, Chinese seal cutting was included in *The Representative List of the Oral and Intangible Heritage of Humanity* by the UNESCO for its active role in protecting and passing on China's fine traditional culture.

篆刻是一种独特的艺术形式,将书法、章法和刀法完美地结合在一起。2009年,中国篆刻因其对保护和传承中国优秀传统文化发挥了积极作用而被联合国教科文组织列入《人类非物质文化遗产代表作名录》。

Seal cutting is carved with materials such as copper, stone, gold, jade, wood, tooth, bone, brick, **plexiglass**② products, and so on, among which the stone is the main material. Besides, the calligraphy of seal cutting mainly adopts oracle bone inscriptions, bronze inscriptions, Warring States inscriptions, large seal characters and small seal characters.

篆刻是用铜、石、金、玉、木、牙、骨、砖、有机玻璃等雕刻而成，其中石材为主要材料。此外，篆刻书法主要采用甲骨文、金文、战国文、大篆和小篆。

佳句点睛 Punchlines

1. The art of seal cutting is mainly used to make seals by combining calligraphy and **engraving**③.

篆刻艺术主要是指用书法与雕刻相结合的方式制作印章。

2. Seal cutting is the concentrated embodiment of the spirit of Chinese national culture, seal is now acting as **stationery**④ printed on the document to indicate **identity**⑤ or signature.

篆刻是中国民族文化精神的集中体现，印章现在作为一种文具，可以在文件上表明身份或签名。

3. Seal cutting plays a positive role in protecting and inheriting China's excellent traditional culture.

篆刻对保护和传承中华优秀传统文化起到了积极作用。

民俗文化

情景对话 Situational Dialogue

A: Hi.

B: Hi. Welcome to my birthday party.

A: Thank you. This is my birthday gift for you. It is a Chinese seal carving with your name engraved on it. I hope you will like it.

B: Oh, wonderful. I like it very much. It looks like a classic gift with Chinese characteristics.

A: You're right. The art of seal cutting is mainly used to make seals by combining calligraphy with engraving, symbolizing power and status.

B: Incredible[⑥]. I love this lovely little gift. Can you tell me more about it?

A: Seal cutting is carved with materials such as copper, stone, gold, jade, wood, tooth, bone, brick, plexiglass products, and so on, among which the stone is the main material. Besides, the calligraphy of seal cutting mainly adopts oracle bone inscriptions, bronze inscriptions, Warring States inscriptions, large seal characters and small seal characters.

B: I feel very honored to own this precious seal cutting with my own Chinese name on it.

A: 你好。

B: 你好。欢迎来到我的生日聚会。

A: 谢谢。这是我送你的生日礼物,是一个中国篆刻,上面刻有你的名字,希望你能喜欢。

B: 噢,太棒了。我非常喜欢它,看起来是一个具有中国特色的经典礼物。

A: 你说对了。篆刻艺术主要是通过书法和雕刻相结合而制作印章的艺术,象征着权力和地位。

B: 难以置信。我很喜欢这个可爱的小礼物。你能告诉我更多的信息吗?

A: 篆刻的制作材料主要是铜、石、金、玉、木、牙、骨、砖、有机玻璃制品等,其中以石材为主。此外,篆刻书法主要采用古文字,包括甲骨文、金文、战国文、大篆和小篆。

B: 能拥有这枚刻有我中文名的珍贵印章,我感到很荣幸。

生词注解　Notes

① symbolize /ˈsɪmbəlaɪz/　*vt.* 象征;用符号表现

② plexiglass /ˈpleksɪɡlɑːs/　*n.* 有机玻璃;塑胶玻璃

③ engrave /ɪnˈɡreɪv/　*vt.* 雕刻

④ stationery /ˈsteɪʃənrɪ/　*n.* 文具;信纸

⑤ identity /aɪˈdentətɪ/　*n.* 身份;同一性

⑥ incredible /ɪnˈkredəbl/　*adj.* 难以置信的;极好的

刺绣

Embroidery

 导入语 Lead-in

刺绣是中国民间传统手工艺之一，古代称为"针绣"，是用针线在织物上绣制出的各种装饰图案的总称，分为丝绣、发绣和羽毛绣。中国刺绣有苏绣、湘绣、蜀绣和粤绣，其中苏绣最负盛名。苏绣图案秀丽、色彩淡雅、针法灵活、绣工细致，兼具装饰性与实用性。刺绣的工艺特征为顺、齐、平、匀、洁。刺绣针法有齐针、套针、扎针、长短针、打子针等。刺绣物品主要用于生活装饰和艺术装饰，如服装、床上用品、台布、舞台、艺术品等。刺绣品的图案多有喜庆、长寿、吉祥之意，深受人们喜爱。享有盛名的刺绣大家有丁佩、沈寿等。

文化剪影 Cultural Outline

Embroidery is one of the traditional folk **crafts**① in ancient China with a history of more than two thousand years. Embroidery refers to the general term for various **decorative**② patterns embroidered in the **fabric**③ with needle and thread, divided into silk embroidery and feather embroidery.

刺绣是中国古代民间传统工艺之一，具有两千多年的历史。刺绣是用针线绣在织物上的各种装饰图案的总称，分为丝绣和羽毛绣。

Chinese embroidery includes Su Embroidery, Xiang Embroidery, Shu Embroidery and Yue Embroidery. Among them, Su Embroidery is the most famous for its unique style of beautiful pattern, elegant color, **flexible**④ stitching and **meticulous**⑤ embroidery, as well as its decorative and practical features.

中国刺绣有苏绣、湘绣、蜀绣和粤绣。其中，苏绣最负盛名，苏绣图案秀丽、色彩淡雅、针法灵活、绣工细致，兼具装饰性与实用性。

The pattern of embroidery is mostly focusing on the meaning of celebration, **longevity**⑥ and **auspiciousness**⑦, are mainly used for life and art decorations, such as clothing, bedding, tablecloth, stage, art, and so on. As a result, embroidery is one of the representatives of Chinese traditional culture and art.

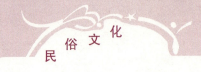

刺绣品的图案多有喜庆、长寿、吉祥等寓意，主要用于服装、床上用品、桌布、舞台、艺术品等生活和艺术装饰，是中国传统文化艺术的代表之一。

 佳句点睛　Punchlines

1. Embroidery refers to the general term for various decorative patterns embroidered in the fabric with needle and thread.

刺绣是用针线绣在织物上的各种装饰图案的总称。

2. The patterns of embroidery items are mostly focusing on the meaning of celebration, longevity and auspiciousness, mainly used for life and art decoration.

刺绣品的图案多有喜庆、长寿、吉祥等寓意，主要用于生活和艺术装饰。

3. Embroidery is one of the representatives of traditional Chinese culture and art, deeply loved by people and enjoying a high reputation at home and abroad.

刺绣是中国传统文化艺术的代表之一，深受人们喜爱，在国内外享有盛誉。

情景对话 Situational Dialogue

A: Hi.

B: Hi. Your new coat is very nice and **classy**®. The pattern on it looks elegant and delicate. Is it printed on it?

A: No. It is embroidery, a needlework. It is divided into silk embroidery and feather embroidery, a general term for all kinds of decorative patterns embroidered on fabrics by needlework.

B: Sounds amazing. I love the needlework. Can you tell me more about embroidery?

A: Of course. Embroidery patterns are mainly focused on festive, longevity and good luck, mainly for life and art decorations.

B: Superb! How many kinds of embroidery are there?

A: Chinese embroidery mainly includes Su Embroidery, Xiang Embroidery, Shu Embroidery and Yue Embroidery.

B: After hearing your introduction, I also wanna buy a coat with embroidery.

A: You'd better go to Wanda **Plaza**®, where there is a shop of embroidery.

B: That's great. Thank you.

A: 你好。

B: 你好。你的新大衣非常好看,很有范儿。大衣的图案看起来

优雅精致,是不是印在上面的?

A:不是,这是刺绣,一种针线活。刺绣分为丝绸刺绣和羽毛刺绣,是用针线绣在布料上的各种装饰图案的总称。

B:听起来很了不起。我非常喜欢这件针织刺绣,你能多讲讲刺绣吗?

A:当然能,刺绣品的图案多有喜庆、长寿、吉祥等寓意,主要用于生活和艺术装饰。

B:棒极了。刺绣有多少种啊?

A:中国刺绣主要有苏绣、湘绣、蜀绣和粤绣。

B:听了你的介绍,我也想买一件刺绣大衣。

A:你最好去万达广场,那里有一家刺绣店。

B:太好了,谢谢你。

生词注解 Notes

① craft /krɑːft/ n. 工艺;手艺

② decorative /ˈdekərətɪv/ adj. 装饰性的;作装饰用的

③ fabric /ˈfæbrɪk/ n. 织物;布料

④ flexible /ˈfleksəbl/ adj. 灵活的;柔韧的

⑤ meticulous /məˈtɪkjələs/ adj. 细致的;细心的

⑥ longevity /lɒnˈdʒevətɪ/ n. 长寿;持久

⑦ auspiciousness /ɔːˈspɪʃəsnəs/ n. 吉祥;吉利

⑧ classy /ˈklæsɪ/ adj. 有品位的;上等的

⑨ plaza /ˈplɑːzə/ n. 购物中心;(西班牙城镇的)广场

陶瓷

Ceramics

导入语 Lead-in

陶瓷文化历史悠久、源远流长，是中华文明史的一个重要组成部分。陶瓷是陶器和瓷器的总称。中国是世界上最早应用陶器的国家之一，瓷器的发明是中国古代劳动人民对人类文明的一项重大贡献。陶与瓷的区别在于使用不同的材料和温度，在制陶的温度基础上再添火加温，陶就变成了瓷。从陶器到瓷器的演变经历了数千年的发展和改进，原始瓷器才被成功烧制。英文中的"china"既有"中国"的意思，又有"陶瓷"的意思，这清楚地表明中国就是"陶瓷的故乡"。具有广泛影响力的陶瓷有江西景德镇陶瓷、浙江龙泉青瓷、江苏宜兴紫砂陶和福建德化白瓷等。

 文化剪影 Cultural Outline

Ceramics①, which is a general term for **pottery**② and **porcelain**③, has made great contributions to the history of human civilization. China is one of the countries in the world to use pottery early, and "china" in English refers to both China and ceramics, which clearly indicates that China is the home of ceramics.

陶瓷是陶器和瓷器的总称，对人类文明史做出了重大贡献。中国是世界上较早使用陶器的国家之一，"china"在英语中既指"中国"又指"陶瓷"，这清楚地表明中国是"陶瓷的故乡"。

Ceramic art is the **crystallization**④ of art and science, of which the most representative works are **Terracotta**⑤ Warriors and Tang Tricolor Glazed Pottery. In addition, the most influential place of production is Jingdezhen in Jiangxi Province, where abound in blue and white porcelain, color glaze porcelain, famille-rose porcelain and rice-pattern decorated porcelain.

陶瓷艺术是艺术与科学的结晶，其中最具代表性的陶瓷作品是兵马俑和唐三彩。此外，最有影响力的陶瓷产地是江西省景德镇，那里盛产青花瓷、颜色釉瓷、粉彩瓷和玲珑瓷。

After thousands of years's development and improvement, the original porcelain was successfully made by adding fire and heating. Every piece of ceramic work has the **dual**[⑥] cultural characteristics of material and spirit, which is highly praised by the world with high **practicability**[⑦] and artistry.

经过几千年的发展和完善,原始瓷器通过加火和加热的方式烧制而成。每件陶瓷作品都有物质和精神的双重文化特征,具有很高的实用性和艺术性,在世界上享有盛誉。

佳句点睛　Punchlines

1. Ceramics, which is the general term for pottery and porcelain, has made significant contributions to the history of human civilization.

陶瓷是陶器和瓷器的总称,对人类文明史做出了重大贡献。

2. Ceramic art is the crystallization of art and science, whose most representative art of works are the Terracotta Warriors and the Tang Tri-colored Glazed Pottery.

陶瓷艺术是艺术和科学的结晶,最具代表性的陶瓷作品有兵马俑和唐三彩。

3. Every piece of ceramic work has the dual cultural characteristics of material and spirit with high practicability and artistry.

每件陶瓷作品都具有物质与精神的双重文化特征,具有很高的实用性和艺术性。

情景对话 Situational Dialogue

A: Where are you going on the summer vacation?

B: Oh, I intend to go to Jingdezhen, Jiangxi Province. It is a place famous for its ceramics with a long history. I wanna buy a set of tableware for my friends.

A: Superb. What else do you know about ceramics? It is a representative of traditional Chinese culture, isn't it?

B: Sure, every piece of ceramic work has high practicability and artistry. Moreover, China is one of the countries in the world to use pottery early and also the hometown of ceramics. Therefore, I advise you to visit there if you wanna have a further knowledge of Chinese culture.

A: Many thanks. After hearing your explanation, I have a certain understanding of ceramics, which is really very attractive.

B: If you like it, you can go to a certain ceramic shop in our city to experience the making of ceramics.

A: Good idea. I will go there when I'm free. Have a good time on your summer vacation.

B: OK. Thank you. Same to you.

A: 你准备去哪里过暑假啊?

B: 噢,我打算去江西省景德镇,那里以陶瓷闻名,历史悠久。我想在那里给朋友买一套餐具。

A：棒极了。关于陶瓷你还知道些什么呢？陶瓷是中国传统文化的代表,对吧？

B：当然,每件陶瓷作品都有很高的实用性和艺术性。更重要的是,中国是世界上较早使用陶器的国家之一,也是陶瓷的故乡。因此,如果你想进一步了解中国文化,建议你也去那里参观一下。

A：多谢。听了你的介绍,我对陶瓷有了一定的了解,陶瓷真的很有魅力。

B：如果你喜欢,你可以去我们城市的陶瓷店体验一下制作陶瓷的过程。

A：好主意。我有空就去那里体验一下。祝你暑假愉快。

B：好的,谢谢,暑假愉快。

生词注解　Notes

① ceramics /səˈræmɪks/　n. 陶瓷制品;陶瓷器

② pottery /ˈpɒtərɪ/　n.（尤指手工制的）陶器;陶土

③ porcelain /ˈpɔːsəlɪn/　n. 瓷;瓷器

④ crystallization /ˌkrɪstəlaɪˈzeɪʃn/　n. 结晶(作用、过程);结晶体

⑤ terracotta /ˌterəˈkɒtə/　n. 赤陶;赤土色

⑥ dual /ˈdjuːəl/　adj. 双的;双重的

⑦ practicability /ˌpræktɪkəˈbɪlətɪ/　n. 实用性;实践性

剪纸

Paper-cut

导入语　Lead-in

中国的剪纸也称"刻纸",是一种用剪刀或刻刀在纸上剪刻花纹,并让人在视觉上具有透空感和艺术享受的镂空艺术,也是中国古老的民间艺术之一。剪纸主要表达了人们对风调雨顺、社会安定和家庭美满的期盼和祝福,是一种用于生活装饰或其他各种民俗活动的民间艺术。不同地区有不同的剪纸艺术风格,其中陕西剪纸有"活化石"之称,完整地传承了中华民族的优秀哲学思想与文化智慧。2006年,剪纸艺术被国务院列入《第一批国家级非物质文化遗产名录》。2009年,中国剪纸被联合国教科文组织列入《人类非物质文化遗产代表作名录》。

文化剪影　Cultural Outline

　　Chinese paper-cut, also known as engraved paper, has a long history with a unique style and a broad mass base, deeply loved by people at home and abroad. Paper-cut is a kind of hollow-out art, using scissors or carving knife to cut patterns on paper and giving people the **visual**① enjoyment of art.

　　中国剪纸又称"刻纸",其历史悠久,风格独特,群众基础广泛,深受国内外人民的喜爱。剪纸是一种镂空艺术,利用剪刀或刻刀在纸上剪刻图案,给人以视觉上的艺术享受。

　　Paper-cut is mainly a kind of folk art used in life decoration or other folk activities. There are different styles of paper-cut art in different areas, among which Shaanxi paper-cut is known as "living **fossil**② ", completely inheriting the excellent **philosophy**③ and cultural wisdom of the Chinese nation.

　　剪纸主要是一种用于生活装饰或其他民俗活动的民间艺术。不同地区的剪纸艺术风格各异,其中陕西剪纸被称为"活化石",它完整地传承了中华民族的优秀哲学思想和文化智慧。

　　Paper-cut mainly conveys people's expectations and blessings for the country's **favorable**④ weather, social stability and harmony, and family happiness. As a result, people put up paper cuts on walls, windows and doors at wedding ceremonies or festivals to **enhance**⑤ the

happy atmosphere.

剪纸主要传达了人们对风调雨顺、社会安定、家庭美满的期盼和祝福。因此,人们在婚礼或节日期间往墙壁、门窗上贴剪纸,以增强喜悦的气氛。

 ## 佳句点睛 Punchlines

1. Paper-cut is used at wedding ceremonies or festivals to enhance the happy atmosphere.

剪纸被用于婚礼或节日,以增强喜悦的气氛。

2. Paper-cut is a kind of hollow-out art, using scissors or carving knife to cut patterns on paper and giving people the visual enjoyment of art.

剪纸是一种镂空艺术,利用剪刀或刻刀在纸上剪刻图案,给人以视觉上的艺术享受。

3. Paper-cut is mainly a kind of folk art used in life decoration or other folk activities, embodying the cultural wisdom of the Chinese nation.

剪纸主要是一种用于生活装饰或其他民俗活动的民间艺术,体现了中华民族的文化智慧。

情景对话 Situational Dialogue

A: Hi, Lily.

B: Hi, Linda. Which club class have you chosen this semester?

A: I haven't decided yet. Can you offer me some suggestions?

B: What do you wanna learn from your ideal club?

A: I wanna learn something about traditional handicrafts embodying the typical Chinese culture with distinctive characteristics.

B: I see. Paper-cut, I think, is a better choice for you.

A: Really? I have little knowledge of paper-cut. Can you tell me something about it?

B: Sure, paper-cut is a kind of hollow-out art, using scissors or carving knife to cut patterns on paper, giving people the visual enjoyment of art. Moreover, paper-cut mainly conveys people's expectations and blessings for the country's favorable weather, social stability and harmony, and family happiness.

A: Great! Is it difficult for me to learn?

B: It's not too difficult. You're so smart that you can surely master the **gist**⑥ of the skill soon.

A: 你好,莉莉。

B: 你好,琳达。这学期你选了什么社团课啊?

A: 我还没决定,你能给我一些建议吗?

民俗文化

B: 你希望从所选的社团中学到什么东西呢?

A: 我想了解一些能够体现中国特色文化的传统手工艺品。

B: 明白了,我认为剪纸是一个不错的选择。

A: 真的吗? 我对剪纸不太了解,你能给我讲讲吗?

B: 当然,剪纸是一种镂空艺术,利用剪刀或刻刀在纸上剪刻图案,给人以视觉上的艺术享受。此外,剪纸主要传达了人们对风调雨顺、社会安定、家庭美满的期盼和祝福。

A: 太好了! 剪纸难学吗?

B: 不太难。你很聪明,一定能迅速掌握要领。

生词注解　Notes

① visual /ˈvɪʒuəl/　*adj.* 视觉的;外表的

② fossil /ˈfɒsl/　*n.* 化石

③ philosophy /fəˈlɒsəfɪ/　*n.* 哲理;哲学

④ favorable /ˈfeɪvərəbl/　*adj.* 有利的;赞许的

⑤ enhance /ɪnˈhɑːns/　*vt.* 提高;增强

⑥ gist /dʒɪst/　*n.* 要点;主旨

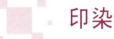

印染

Printing and Dyeing

导入语　Lead-in

印染，古称"染整"，主要是指对纤维、纱线和织物等纺织材料进行化学加工处理的工艺过程，包括前处理、染色、印花、后整理和洗水等。印染的染料主要是矿物染料和植物染料。经过印染的纺织品不但颜色丰富、色彩亮丽，而且不易褪色。从印染工艺上来说，最具代表性的是印染、蜡染和扎染。中国民间印染历史悠久、方法多样，不同地区形成了不同的印染风格，比如鲁西南的织锦、湘西的蓝印花布和维吾尔族的印花布等。印染题材多为花草、人物和故事传说等，大都寄托了人们对美好生活的向往。印染艺术不仅具有实用价值，而且颇具审美价值。

文化剪影 Cultural Outline

Printing and dyeing mainly refer to the chemical processing of textile materials, such as fiber, yarn, fabric, and so on. The art of printing and dyeing is not only of practical value, but also of **aesthetic**① value, which vividly reflects the simple and profound cultural and artistic **deposits**②.

印染主要是指对纤维、纱线、织物等纺织材料的化学加工过程，其方法和技术多种多样。印染艺术既具有实用价值，又颇具审美价值，生动展现了朴素而深厚的文化艺术底蕴。

China's printing and dyeing handiwork is **prevalent**③ now as a folk handicraft, which falls into different schools in accordance with its own local style, for instance, **brocade**④ produced from southwest Shandong, printed blue cotton produced from west Hunan and printed fabrics made by Uyghur, and so on. In terms of printing and dyeing techniques, the most representative methods are printing and dyeing, wax-dyeing and tie-dyeing.

中国民间印染工艺如今依然极为盛行，各地因其不同的印染风格而自成流派，比如鲁西南的织锦、湘西的蓝印花布、维吾尔族的印花布等。从印染工艺上来说，最具代表性的是印染、蜡染和扎染。

Most of the patterns used in Chinese printing and dyeing have rich folk colors, and the subjects are mostly flowers, characters, stories and legends. Most of them **entrust**⑤ people's longing for a better life. In modern urban life, the folk printing and dyeing process with **distinctive**⁶ local characteristics and traditional cultural meaning has won more and more people's love.

中国印染采用的图案多带有浓郁的民间色彩,题材多为花草、人物和故事传说等,大都寄托了人们对美好生活的向往。在现代都市生活中,具有鲜明地方特色和传统文化意蕴的民间印染工艺赢得了越来越多人的喜爱。

佳句点睛 Punchlines

1. Printing and dyeing reflect the simple and profound cultural and artistic deposits.

印染展现了朴素而深厚的文化艺术底蕴。

2. China's printing and dyeing handiwork falls into different schools in accordance with its own local style.

中国的印染工艺按照各地风格分为不同的流派。

3. China's printing and dyeing convey people's aspiration for beautiful life by virtue of its distinctive local feature and traditional cultural **implication**⁷.

中国印染以鲜明的地方特色和传统文化意蕴表达了人们对美好生活的向往。

情景对话 Situational Dialogue

A: I saw you reading a book in the library yesterday morning. What was it?

B: Oh, it is a book on printing and dyeing, which is my professional book.

A: Wow, you seemed to be buried in it when reading. Can you say something about that book?

B: Of course, printing and dyeing, with a history of more than six thousand years, mainly refer to the process of chemical processing of textile materials. It is prevalent now as a folk handicraft, falling into different schools in accordance with its own local styles.

A: Awesome[⑧]. It means that you will find a **relevant**[⑨] job after graduation?

B: Sure, I love traditional Chinese culture and printing and dyeing reflects the simple and profound cultural and artistic accumulation with distinctive local feature. I hope I can make contributions to the development and inheritance of traditional Chinese culture.

A: Thank you for your vivid account. Wonderful!

B: Thank you for your **acclaims**[⑩]. I will try my best to improve myself.

A: 昨天早上我看见你在图书馆看书,是什么书啊?

B：噢，这是一本关于印染的书，是我的专业书。

A：哇，你看书的时候好像很专注啊，能说说那本书吗？

B：当然。印染已有六千多年的历史了，主要是指纺织材料的化学加工过程，经过印染加工的民间手工艺品现在非常流行，按照各地风格分为不同的流派。

A：太棒了。这意味着你毕业后会找到一份相关的工作？

B：当然，我热爱中国传统文化，印染反映了淳朴深厚的文化艺术积淀，具有鲜明的地方特色，我希望能为中国传统文化的发展和传承做出贡献。

A：谢谢你生动的介绍。太棒了！

B：谢谢你的赞扬，我会努力提升自己的。

生词注解 Notes

① aesthetic /iːsˈθetɪk/ adj. 审美的；艺术的

② deposit /dɪˈpɒzɪt/ n. 沉积物；矿床

③ prevalent /ˈprevələnt/ adj. 流行的；盛行的

④ brocade /brəˈkeɪd/ n. 织锦缎；(尤指用金银线织出凸纹的)厚织物

⑤ entrust /ɪnˈtrʌst/ vt. 委托；信托

⑥ distinctive /dɪˈstɪŋktɪv/ adj. 有特色的；与众不同的

⑦ implication /ˌɪmplɪˈkeɪʃn/ n. 含意；暗指

⑧ awesome /ˈɔːsəm/ adj. 棒极了的；极好的

⑨ relevant /ˈreləvənt/ adj. 相关的；切题的

⑩ acclaim /əˈkleɪm/ n. 赞誉；高度评价

景泰蓝

Cloisonné

导入语 Lead-in

景泰蓝，也称"铜胎掐丝珐琅"或"嵌珐琅"，因其在明朝景泰年间的制作工艺水平达到了顶峰，而且所用珐琅釉多以蓝色为主，故名"景泰蓝"。景泰蓝制作原料主要为紫铜和珐琅，产品外观精美、色彩夺目，给人一种古典高雅、繁花似锦的艺术感受。景泰蓝诞生于北京，以造型典雅、纹样丰富、色彩华丽庄重而闻名于世，它既是皇宫大殿的重要装饰品，也是集美术、铸造、工艺、雕刻、镶嵌、玻璃熔制和冶金等于一体的综合性工艺，体现了鲜明的民族风格和深厚的文化内涵，是具有北京特色的传统手工艺品之一，也是中国金属工艺品中的重要品种。1904年，中国景泰蓝荣获圣路易斯世博会头奖。2006年被国务院列入《第一批国家级非物质文化遗产名录》。

文化剪影　Cultural Outline

Cloisonné, is a famous traditional handicraft in Beijing and an important variety of Chinese metal crafts. It was known as Cloisonné, which was mainly made of copper and **enamel**[①], in that its production technology in Jingtai period of the Ming Dynasty reached the peak while the enamel was mostly blue.

景泰蓝是北京著名的传统手工艺品,也是中国金属工艺品的重要品种。因其在明代景泰年间的制作工艺水平达到了顶峰,而且所用珐琅釉多以蓝色为主,故名"景泰蓝"。

Produced in Beijing, Cloisonné is famous for its elegant shape, rich patterns, **gorgeous**[②] and solemn colors, giving people an artistic feeling of classical elegance and flowers blooming like a piece of brocade and reflecting a **distinctive**[③] national style and profound cultural **connotation**[④].

景泰蓝产于北京,以造型典雅、纹样丰富、色彩华丽庄重而著称,给人以古典高雅、繁花似锦的艺术感受,体现了鲜明的民族风格和深厚的文化内涵。

Cloisonné is not only an important **ornament**[⑤] of the palace hall, but also a comprehensive technological integrating art, casting, technology, sculpture, **inlay**[⑥], glass melting, **metallurgy**[⑦] and other technologies, which is one of the traditional handicrafts with Beijing characteristics.

景泰蓝不仅是宫廷殿堂的重要装饰品,还是集艺术、铸造、工艺、雕刻、镶嵌、玻璃熔制、冶金等技术于一体的综合性工艺,是具有北京特色的传统手工艺品之一。

佳句点睛　Punchlines

1. Cloisonné, is a famous traditional handicraft in Beijing and an important variety of Chinese metal crafts, with a certain historical status and significance.

景泰蓝是北京著名的传统手工艺品,是中国金属工艺的重要品种,具有一定的历史地位和意义。

2. Cloisonné is famous for its elegant shape, rich patterns, gorgeous colors and solemnity, giving people an artistic feeling of classical elegance and flowers blooming like a piece of brocade.

景泰蓝以造型典雅、纹样丰富、色彩华丽庄重而著称,给人以古典高雅、繁花似锦的艺术感受。

3. Cloisonné is one of the traditional handicrafts in Beijing and also an important decoration for the palace.

景泰蓝是具有北京特色的传统手工艺品之一,也是宫廷的重要装饰品。

情景对话 Situational Dialogue

A: Hi, Lily.

B: Hi, Helen. What do you intend to do at the coming weekend?

A: I plan to go to an **antique**® market to pick out a piece of Cloisonné to be a New Year gift for my grandpa.

B: I don't know much about Cloisonné. Can you tell me something about it?

A: Definitely, it was known as **Cloisonné**, in that its production technology in Jingtai period of Ming Dynasty reached the peak while the enamel was mostly blue.

B: Awesome! Is it one of the traditional handicrafts with Beijing characteristics?

A: Yes, Cloisonné is a famous traditional handicraft in Beijing. Besides, **Cloisonné** is famous for its elegant shape, rich patterns, gorgeous and solemn colors, which was used as an important ornament of the palace.

B: I'd like to have a chance to see it in person.

A: 你好,莉莉。

B: 你好,海伦。这周末准备做什么啊?

A: 我打算去古玩市场挑选一件景泰蓝作为新年礼物送给爷爷。

B: 我对景泰蓝不太了解。你能给我讲讲吗?

A: 当然。明朝景泰年间,景泰蓝的生产工艺水平达到了顶峰,而且所用珐琅釉多以蓝色为主,故名"景泰蓝"。

B: 太棒了,它是北京特色的传统手工艺品之一吗?

A: 是的,景泰蓝是北京著名的传统手工艺品,以造型典雅、纹样丰富、色彩华丽庄重而闻名,是宫殿的重要装饰品。

B: 我希望有机会去亲眼看看。

 ## 生词注解 Notes

① enamel /ɪˈnæml/ *n.* 珐琅;搪瓷

② gorgeous /ˈɡɔːdʒəs/ *adj.* 非常漂亮的;令人愉快的

③ distinctive /dɪˈstɪŋktɪv/ *adj.* 有特色的;与众不同的

④ connotation /ˌkɒnəˈteɪʃn/ *n.* 内涵;含蓄

⑤ ornament /ˈɔːnəmənt/ *n.* 装饰品;装饰

⑥ inlay /ˌɪnˈleɪ/ *n.* 镶嵌艺术;镶嵌装饰或图案

⑦ metallurgy /məˈtælədʒɪ/ *n.* 冶金;冶金学

⑧ antique /ænˈtiːk/ *adj.* 古老的;古董的

中国结

Chinese Knot

导入语 Lead-in

中国结始于中国古人的结绳记事,是中国特有的民间手工编结艺术。中国结从头到尾都由一根丝线编结而成,不仅造型优美、色彩多样,而且寓意深刻、内涵丰富,象征团结一致、永结同心,表达了人们追求真、善、美的良好愿望和对美好事物的感恩与祝福。作为中国传统文化的象征,中国结和中国的戏曲、书画、美食、乐器、剪纸一样,彰显了中国独特的东方神韵。作为中国传统的吉祥装饰物品,中国结给人带来团圆、亲密、和谐、温馨的美好感受,是炎黄子孙心连心的象征。"结"与"吉"谐音,"吉"有福、禄、寿、喜、财、安、康等寓意,是人类追求的永恒主

题,体现了中国传统文化的精髓和中国人民的智慧,深受各国朋友喜爱。

 文化剪影　Cultural Outline

The Chinese knot is a unique folk hand knitting art in China with a long history, made up of one silk thread from the beginning to the end. The Chinese knot is beautiful in shape, colorful, rich in connotation and **profound**[①] in meaning, deeply loved by friends from all over the world.

中国结是中国历史悠久的民间手工编织艺术,由一根丝线自始至终编织而成。中国结造型优美、色彩多样、内涵丰富、意义深远,深受各国朋友的喜爱。

As a symbol of traditional Chinese culture, the Chinese knot showcases the unique **oriental**[②] charm of China like Chinese operas, calligraphy and painting, **cuisine**[③], musical instruments and paper-cut, highlighting the essence of traditional Chinese culture and the wisdom of Chinese people.

作为中国传统文化的象征,中国结与戏曲、书画、美食、乐器、剪纸一样,展现了中国独特的东方神韵,彰显了中国传统文化的精髓和中华民族的智慧。

As a traditional Chinese **auspicious**[④] jewelry, Chinese knot brings people a happy feeling of reunion, closeness, harmony and warmth. In addition, "knot" and "luck" are **homophonic**⑤ in Chinese, and the latter means happiness, wealth, **longevity**⑥, security, and so on, which is the **eternal**⑦ theme of human pursuit.

作为中国传统的吉祥饰品，中国结给人带来团圆、亲密、和谐、温馨的幸福感受。此外，"结"与"吉"谐音，"吉"有福、财、寿、安等寓意，是人类追求的永恒主题。

佳句点睛　Punchlines

1. The Chinese knot is a unique folk hand knitting art in China with a long history, profound meaning and rich connotation.

中国结是我国历史悠久的独特民间手工编织艺术，意义深远，内涵丰富。

2. As a symbol of traditional Chinese culture, the Chinese knot showcases the unique oriental charm of and the wisdom of Chinese people.

作为中国传统文化的象征，中国结展现了中国特有的东方魅力和中国人民的智慧。

3. As a traditional Chinese auspicious ornament, Chinese knot brings people a happy feeling of reunion, intimacy, harmony and warmth.

作为中国传统的吉祥饰品，中国结给人带来一种团圆、亲密、和谐、温馨的幸福感受。

 情景对话 Situational Dialogue

A: Hi, Anna. Welcome to my house.

B: Hi, Meilan. Thanks for your invitation. Your home is so warm and cozy that I'm deeply impressed. There seems to be a beautiful and attractive red object hanging on the wall of every living room in China. What is it?

A: It is a Chinese knot, made up of one silk thread from the beginning to the end, revealing the essence of traditional Chinese culture and the wisdom of Chinese people.

B: Superb. Why do you hang it in your living room?

A: Well, as a traditional Chinese auspicious ornament, the Chinese knot brings people a happy feeling of reunion, intimacy, harmony and warmth. As a result, it is common for us Chinese people to hang it in the living room to pray for a healthy and happy life.

B: I see. The Chinese knot is a symbol of traditional Chinese culture.

A: You're right. If you like it, I can make a Chinese knot for you.

B: Really? You are so **considerate**⑧ and thoughtful. Thank you very much.

A: 你好，安娜。欢迎来我家做客。

B: 你好，梅兰。谢谢你的邀请，你的家温馨舒适，令我印象深刻。在中国,家家户户客厅的墙上似乎都挂着一件既漂亮又引人注目的红色物件。这是什么啊?

A:这是中国结,由一根丝线从头到尾编结而成,显示了中国传统文化的精髓和中国人民的智慧。

B:很不错噢,你们为什么把它挂在客厅里啊?

A:作为中国传统吉祥饰品,中国结给人带来团圆、亲密、和谐、温馨的幸福感受。因此,中国人常把它挂在客厅里,以祈求健康、快乐的生活。

B:我懂了,中国结是中国传统文化的一种象征。

A:你说对了,如果你喜欢,我可以给你编一个中国结。

B:真的吗? 你太好了,非常感谢。

生词注解　Notes

① profound /prəˈfaʊnd/　adj. 深厚的;意义深远的

② oriental /ˌɔːriˈentl/　n. 东方的;东方人的

③ cuisine /kwɪˈziːn/　n. 美食;中餐

④ auspicious /ɔːˈspɪʃəs/　adj. 吉祥的;吉利的

⑤ homophonic /ˌhɒməˈfɒnɪk/　adj. 同音的;同音异义的

⑥ longevity /lɒnˈdʒevəti/　n. 长寿;长命

⑦ eternal /ɪˈtɜːnl/　adj. 永恒的;永久的

⑧ considerate /kənˈsɪdərət/　adj. 体贴的;考虑周到的

风筝

Kites

导入语　Lead-in

风筝产生于春秋战国时期。相传，古代哲学家墨翟以鸟为形，以木为料，制作出可以飞行的"木鸢"，这就是风筝的起源。在中国古代，木鸢一直是战争时传递信息的重要工具和携带火药作战进攻的军事武器。经过漫长的历史演变，放风筝已经成为一项深爱人们喜爱的户外活动。风筝设计精致、图案丰富、构思巧妙、趣味盎然，富有独特的格调和浓烈的民族色彩。同时，受中国传统文化的熏陶，风筝的图案大多寓意吉祥，表现了人们对美好生活的向往和憧憬。山东潍坊是中国著名的风筝产地，被誉为"世界风筝之都"。2006年，潍坊风筝制作技艺被国务院列入《第一批国家级非物质文化遗产名录》。

文化剪影　Cultural Outline

Kites, which originated in the Spring and Autumn Period and the Warring States Period, was made of wood in the shape of birds invented by Mo Di, an ancient philosopher. After a long history of **advancement**① and **evolution**②, kite-flying has become a favorite outdoor activity.

风筝起源于春秋战国时期,是古代哲学家墨翟发明的鸟形木制品。经过长期的发展演变,放风筝已经成为一项人们喜爱的户外活动。

With the profound traditional Chinese culture, Weifang, Shandong Province has produced a significant number of worldwide famous kites, honored as "The Kite Capital of the World". Kite-making techniques in Weifang was listed in *The First Batchof National* **Intangible**③ *Cultural Heritages* by the State Council in 2006.

山东潍坊拥有深厚的中国传统文化,生产了一大批世界闻名的风筝,被誉为"世界风筝之都"。2006年,潍坊风筝制作技术被国务院列入《第一批国家级非物质文化遗产名录》。

As an important tool for **transmitting**④ information in ancient wars and a military weapon carrying gunpowder for combat attack, kites are exquisitely shaped, richly patterned, skillfully designed, full of interest, unique in style and rich in national color, **signifying**⑤ auspi-

ciousness and showing people's yearning and longing for a better life.

作为古代战争中传递信息的重要工具和携带火药作战进攻的军事武器,风筝形状精美、图案丰富、设计巧妙、趣味盎然、风格独特、民族色彩浓厚、寓意吉祥,表现了人们对美好生活的向往和憧憬。

 佳句点睛　Punchlines

1. According to the legend, the kite was invented by the ancient philosopher Mo Di more than two thousand years ago.

传说,风筝是两千多年前古代哲学家墨翟发明的。

2. The Weifang Kite in Shandong embodies the cultural spirit of the Chinese nation, So Weifang is known as "The Kite Capital of the World".

山东潍坊风筝体现了中华民族的文化精神,潍坊被誉为"世界风筝之都"。

3. The pattern of the kite is auspicious and rich, showing the people's yearning and longing for a better life.

风筝的图案吉祥丰富,表现了人们对美好生活的向往和憧憬。

 情景对话　Situational Dialogue

A: Hi, Lisa.

B: Hi, Mengmeng. What is it in your hand?

A: it is a kite. I plan to fly a kite with my kids an hour later. Do you wanna go with us?

B: Of course, I'd like to go. It looks cute. Can you tell me something about it?

A: Yes, I can. Kites were invented in the shape of birds by Mo Di, an ancient philosopher. Besides, kites were used as a vital tool to **circulate**⑥ information and a military weapon to carry gunpowder in the war of ancient times.

B: Unbelievable, what I wanna say is that kites have such a profound cultural connotation. Do you think it is easy to fly kites?

A: Not too easy. Kite-flying requires skills and weather conditions, such as the windy weather.

B: Today is windy. It is suitable for us to fly kites.

A: By all means. If you're interested in kites, Weifang, Shandong Province, honored as "The Kite Capital of the World", is a place that is worthy visiting.

B: Thank you. Let's go to fly kites together.

A: 你好,丽莎。

B: 你好,蒙蒙。你手里拿的是什么啊?

A: 风筝。我准备一小时后带孩子去放风筝,你要不要一起去啊?

B: 当然,我很乐意,它看起来很可爱,你能给我介绍一下风筝吗?

A: 能。风筝是古代哲学家墨翟依据鸟的形状发明的。此外,风

民俗文化

筝在古代战争中被用作传递信息的重要工具和携带火药的军事武器。

B: 难以置信,风筝有如此深刻的文化内涵。你认为放风筝容易吗?

A: 不太容易,放风筝需要技巧,也要仰仗天气条件,如多风的天气。

B: 今天多风,适合放风筝。

A: 当然。如果你对风筝感兴趣,被誉为"世界风筝之都"的山东潍坊是一个值得去的地方。

B: 谢谢,等会儿我们一起放风筝吧。

生词注解　Notes

① advancement /ədˈvɑːnsmənt/　*n.* 发展;促进

② evolution /ˌiːvəˈluːʃn/　*n.* 演变;进化

③ intangible /ɪnˈtændʒəbl/　*adj.* 无形的

④ transmit /trænzˈmɪt/　*vt.* 传播;传达

⑤ signify /ˈsɪɡnɪfaɪ/　*vt.* 表示;意味

⑥ circulate /ˈsɜːkjəleɪt/　*vt.* 传递;使……循环

第三部分 建 筑

Part Ⅲ Architecture

宫殿

Palace

 导入语　Lead-in

宫殿是皇帝朝会和居住的场所，依托城市并严格按照中轴对称的结构而建，其规模宏大、气势雄伟、设计精巧、装饰豪华，彰显了皇家尊严和皇权的至高无上，凸显了宫殿在整个都城中的地位。宫殿是中国古代建筑的重要组成部分，也是中国古代建筑中最高级、最豪华的建筑。宫殿建筑风格独特，明显区别于其他类型的建筑，是中国传统文化的重要组成部分。北京故宫，旧称"紫禁城"，是中国明清皇家宫殿。目前，故宫是中国现存最完整的古代宫殿建筑群，也是世界上现存规模大、保存完整的木质结构古建筑之一。1987年，北京故宫被联合国教科文组织评为世界文化遗产。

民俗文化

文化剪影　Cultural Outline

The palace was the place where the emperors held morning **assembly**① and lived, mainly depending on the city and strictly following the **symmetrical**② structure of the central **axis**③. In addition, the palace was grand in scale, magnificent in **momentum**④, exquisite in design and **luxurious**⑤ in decoration, showing the dignity of the royal family and the supreme authority of the imperial power, and highlighting the position of the palace in the whole capital city.

宫殿是皇帝朝会和居住的场所，主要依托城市并严格按照中轴对称的结构而建。此外，宫殿规模宏大、气势雄伟、设计精巧、装饰豪华，彰显了皇室尊严和皇权的至高无上，凸显了宫殿在整个都城中的地位。

The Imperial Palace in Beijing, formerly known as "The Forbidden City", is the most complete ancient palace **complex**⑥ in China as well as one of the large wooden ancient buildings existing in the world. In 1987, the Imperial Palace of Beijing was listed as a world cultural heritage by UNESCO.

北京故宫，旧称"紫禁城"，是中国现存最完整的古代宫殿建筑群，也是世界上现存的大型木制古建筑之一。1987年，北京故宫被联合国教科文组织评为世界文化遗产。

The palace is an important part of traditional Chinese culture and ancient **architecture**[7], and its architectural style is unique, which is obviously different from other types of architecture. In addition, the palace is also the most advanced and luxurious building type in ancient Chinese architecture.

宫殿是中国传统文化和古代建筑的重要组成部分，其建筑风格独特，与其他类型的建筑明显不同。此外，宫殿也是中国古代建筑中最高级、最奢华的建筑类型。

佳句点睛　Punchlines

1. The palace is built on the city and strictly in accordance with the symmetrical structure of the central axis, highlighting the dignity of the royal family and the **supremacy**[8] of the imperial power.

宫殿依托城市并严格按照中轴对称的结构而建，彰显了皇室尊严和皇权的至高无上。

2. The Imperial Palace in Beijing, formerly known as "The Forbidden City", is the most complete ancient palace complex in China as well as one of the large existing wooden ancient buildings existing in the world.

北京故宫，原名"紫禁城"，是中国现存最完整的古代宫殿建筑群，也是世界上现存的大型木制古建筑之一。

3. The palace with unique structure is the most advanced and luxu-

rious architectural type in ancient Chinese architecture.

宫殿结构独特，是中国古代建筑中最高级、最豪华的建筑类型。

情景对话 Situational Dialogue

A: Our school is scheduled to held a speech contest related to typical Chinese culture next week. Have you signed up?

B: Yes, I have been preparing for it recently after signing up.

A: What is your topic about the speech?

B: The topic of my speech is the palace, which is usually grand in scale, magnificent in momentum, exquisite in design and luxurious in decoration, highlighting the dignity of the royal family and the supremacy of imperial power.

A: Awesome. Is the Imperial Palace in Beijing a kind of representative palace?

B: Yes. The Imperial Palace in Beijing, formerly known as the Forbidden City, is the most complete ancient palace complex in China as well as one of the large wooden ancient buildings existing in the world.

A: After hearing your vivid explanation, I can hardly wait to hear your speech on the scene.

B: Welcome.

A: 我们学校计划下周举行一场与中国代表性文化有关的演讲

比赛,你报名了吗?

B: 报名了,报名后我一直在准备这场比赛。

A: 你演讲的主题是什么?

B: 我演讲的主题是宫殿,宫殿大都规模宏大、气势雄伟、设计精巧、装饰豪华,彰显了皇室尊严和皇权的至高无上。

A: 太棒了,北京故宫是宫殿的典型代表吧?

B: 是的,北京故宫,旧称"紫禁城",是中国现存最完整的古代宫殿建筑群,也是世界上现存的大型木制古建筑之一。

A: 听了你生动的介绍后,我迫不及待地想去现场听你演讲了。

B: 欢迎。

生词注解 Notes

① assembly /əˈsemblɪ/   *n.* 集会;汇编

② symmetry /ˈsɪmətrɪ/   *n.* 对称;匀称

③ axis /ˈæksɪs/   *n.* 轴;轴线

④ momentum /məˈmentəm/   *n.* 势头;动力

⑤ luxurious /lʌɡˈʒʊərɪəs/   *adj.* 奢侈的;丰富的

⑥ complex /ˈkɒmpleks/   *n.* 建筑群;复合体

⑦ architecture /ˈɑːkɪtektʃə(r)/   *n.* 建筑风格;建筑学

⑧ supremacy /suˈpreməsɪ/   *n.* 至高无上;主权

园林

Gardens

中国园林是中国古代建筑艺术的珍宝。受中国传统文化的影响,中国园林通过地形、山水、建筑群、花木等体现了不同历史时期的精神文化和人文思想,尤其是诗、词、绘画的思想境界。园林按历史可分为古典园林与现代园林;按功能可分为综合园林、动物园、植物园、儿童公园和城市绿地等。其中,在古典园林中,中国园林有皇家园林、私家园林、寺观园林和风景园林。中国园林虽然风格迥异,但都追求人与自然的完美结合,同时把中国特有的书法艺术等文化意境融入其中,彰显园林的文化底蕴。

第三部分　建筑

文化剪影　Cultural Outline

Gardens refer to the **ecological**① environment for people's viewing, **recreation**② and living created by human beings through the terrain, mountains and rivers, buildings, flowers and trees, and so on. Chinese gardens not only inherit the traditional culture, but also play a positive role in urban greening and environmental protection.

园林是指人类通过地形、山水、建筑群、花木等开辟的供人们观赏、游憩、居住的生态环境。中国园林不但继承了传统文化,而且对城市绿化和环境保护起到了积极的作用。

The Chinese classical gardens include imperial gardens such as the Summer Palace, Chengde Summer Mountain Resort, private gardens such as Suzhou Gardens, temple gardens such as Hanshan Temple, and landscape gardens. Chinese gardens pursue the perfect combination of man and nature.

中国古典园林包括颐和园、承德避暑山庄等皇家园林,苏州园林等私家园林,寒山寺等寺观园林以及风景园林。中国园林追求人与自然的完美结合。

Under the influence of traditional Chinese culture, Chinese gardens are the treasures of ancient Chinese architectural art, which integrate the art of **plaques**③, couplets and **tablet**④ inscriptions into the gardens to **highlight**⑤ the cultural deposits of the gardens.

在中国传统文化的影响下，中国园林是中国古代建筑艺术的瑰宝，将匾额、楹联、碑刻艺术等融入造园之中，彰显园林的文化底蕴。

佳句点睛　Punchlines

1. Gardens refer to the ecological environment for people's viewing, recreation and living created by human beings through the terrain, mountains and rivers, buildings, flowers and trees, and so on.

园林是指人类通过地形、山水、建筑群、花木等开辟的供人们观赏、游憩、居住的生态环境。

2. Chinese gardens are divided into different types according to different angles, pursuing the perfect combination of man and nature as well as the elegant cultural connotation.

中国园林按不同的角度分为不同的类型，追求人与自然的完美结合和高雅的文化寓意。

3. Chinese gardens are the unique gem of the Chinese ancient architectural art, **manifesting**⑥ the spiritual culture and the humanistic thoughts in different historical periods.

中国园林是中国古代建筑艺术的瑰宝，体现了不同历史时期的精神文化和人文思想。

情景对话　Situational Dialogue

A: I've heard that you're from Suzhou, which is famous for its gardens, isn't it? Can you share some information about Suzhou Gardens?

B: Suzhou Gardens are private ones, including Canglang Pavilion, Lion Forest, Humble Administrator's Garden, Lingering Garden, and so on, which are exquisitely designed and deeply loved by people at home and abroad.

A: What else do you know about gardens besides Suzhou Gardens?

B: Among the Chinese classical gardens are royal gardens including Summer Palace and Chengde Summer Mountain Resort. In addition, Chinese gardens are the treasure of the ancient Chinese architectural art, such as integrating Chinese unique calligraphy art forms, including plaque, couplet, inscription art, and so on, into the garden, and manifesting the cultural deposits.

A: After hearing your explanation, I long to visit Suzhou Gardens to enjoy their charming scenery.

B: Okay, welcome to my hometown, when I can be your tour guide.

A: That's great. Thank you very much.

B: My pleasure.

民俗文化

A：听说你是苏州人，苏州以园林闻名，对吧？你能介绍一下苏州园林吗？

B：苏州园林属于私家园林，包括沧浪亭、狮子林、拙政园、留园等，设计精致，深受国内外人士的喜爱。

A：除了苏州园林外，你还知道其他园林吗？

B：中国古典园林中有颐和园、承德避暑山庄等皇家园林。此外，中国园林是中国古代建筑艺术的瑰宝，将匾额、楹联、碑刻艺术等融入造园之中，彰显园林的文化底蕴。

A：听完你的介绍，我十分希望能欣赏苏州园林迷人的景色。

B：好啊，欢迎来我的家乡，到时候我可以做导游。

A：太好了！非常感谢。

B：不客气。

生词注解　Notes

① ecological /ˌiːkəˈlɒdʒɪkl/　*adj.* 生态的；生态学的

② recreation /ˌriːkrɪˈeɪʃn/　*n.* 娱乐；消遣

③ plaque /plæk/　*n.* 匾；饰板

④ tablet /ˈtæblət/　*n.* 碑；写字板

⑤ highlight /ˈhaɪlaɪt/　*vt.* 突出；强调

⑥ manifest /ˈmænɪfest/　*vt.* 表明；清楚显示（尤指情感、态度或品质）

北京四合院

Beijing Siheyuan

导入语　Lead-in

北京四合院,又称"四合房",源于汉朝。"四"指东、西、南、北四个方向都建有房屋,即正房(北房)、倒座(南座)、东厢房和西厢房,"合"就是四面房屋围在一起形成一个"口"字形的结构,里面是一个中心庭院,东南方向开一个门,寓意财源滚滚。根据风水学理论,北京四合院一般坐北朝南,四面房屋各自独立,彼此之间由走廊连接,起居方便。四合院中间的庭院空间宽敞,庭院内可以植树栽花、饲鸟养鱼、叠石造景、自成天地,一家人可以在此谈天说地,其乐融融。经过几百年的营建,北京四合院已经形成了特有的京味风格,蕴含着深刻的文化内涵,是中华传统文化的独特载体。

文化剪影　Cultural Outline

Beijing Siheyuan, also known as "Sihefang", originated in the Han Dynasty. "Four" refers to the four houses built in the east, west, south and north directions, namely, the main house (north house), **inverted**① house (south house), east-wing house and west-wing house, which **enclose**② together, forming a mouth-shaped structure, with a courtyard in the center and a door in the southeast direction, and implying that the money keeps rolling in.

北京四合院,又称"四合房",源于汉朝。"四"是指建在东、西、南、北四个方向的房屋,即正房(北房)、倒座(南座)、东厢房和西厢房四座房屋,围合在一起,形成"口"字形结构,中间有庭院,东南方向开一个门,寓意财源滚滚。

According to the theory of fengshui, Beijing Siheyuan generally faces south. The houses in the four directions are independent and connected with each other by corridors, making it convenient for living. In addition, the **spacious**③ courtyard in the middle can be used for planting trees and flowers, feeding birds and fish, and **stacking**④ rocks and landscaping, providing a private environment for family reunion.

根据风水学理论,北京四合院一般坐北朝南。四面房屋各自独立,彼此之间由走廊连接,起居方便。此外,中间的庭院空间宽敞,庭院内可以植树栽花、饲鸟养鱼、叠石造景,为家庭团聚提供了私密环境。

Beijing Siheyuan is an enclosed courtyard, with a unique style. The main house faces south with plenty of light, warmth and comfort. In addition, the layout, internal structure and interior decoration of the courtyard focus on the use of traditional Chinese philosophy and **artifacts**[⑤] with profound cultural connotation to **convey**[⑥] the significance of traditional Chinese culture.

北京四合院庭院封闭,风格独特,主房坐北朝南、光线充足、温暖舒适。此外,庭院的布局、内部结构和室内装饰都注重运用蕴含中国传统哲学和深厚文化内涵的器物,以传达中国传统文化的意义。

佳句点睛 Punchlines

1. Beijing Siheyuan, closed in the middle courtyard, with a door opening in the southeast, implies that the money keeps rolling in.

北京四合院,中间庭院封闭,东南方向开一个门,寓意财源滚滚。

2. According to the theory of fengshui, the main house of Beijing Siheyuan generally faces south, with plenty of light, warmth and comfort.

根据风水学理论,北京四合院的主房一般坐北朝南,光线充足,温暖舒适。

3. The **construction**[⑦] and decoration of Beijing Siheyuan embody the significance of the traditional Chinese culture.

北京四合院的建造和装饰体现了中国传统文化的重要意义。

生词注解 Notes

① inverted /ɪnˈvɜːtɪd/ *adj.* 倒转的；反方向的

② enclose /ɪnˈkləʊz/ *vt.* 围绕；放入封套

③ spacious /ˈspeɪʃəs/ *adj.* 宽敞的；无边无际的

④ stack /stæk/ *vt.* 使……放成整齐的一叠；使……成叠地放在……

⑤ artifact /ˈɑːtɪfækt/ *n.* 人工制品；手工艺品

⑥ convey /kənˈveɪ/ *vt.* 传达；表达

⑦ construction /kənˈstrʌkʃn/ *n.* 建设；建筑物

第三部分　建筑

上海里弄

Shanghai Lilong

导入语　Lead-in

上海里弄，又称"弄堂"，是上海特有的民居形式，与上海人的生活息息相关，既保留了中国传统建筑的痕迹，又受到外来建筑的影响，最能代表近代上海城市文化的特征。上海里弄住宅具有强烈的空间艺术特征，居民的居住空间被分隔成街道、总弄、支弄和住宅内部。这种空间组织方式不仅能让居民产生强烈的地域感、认同感和安全感，而且容易营造出一种氛围浓烈的邻里感和社区感，从而培育和睦亲密的邻里关系。上海里弄包括广式里弄、新式石库门里弄、花园式里弄和新式里弄等，其中新式石库门里弄是具有上海特色的居民住宅之一。里弄既是许多上海人休闲娱乐的主要场所，也是重要

的交易买卖场所,田子坊是上海建筑中最具特色的里弄。

文化剪影　Cultural Outline

Shanghai Lilong, known as "alley", is the most unique and important **residential**① form in Shanghai. Influenced by both traditional Chinese and foreign architecture, Shanghai Lilong is closely related to the life of Shanghai people, representing the characteristics of modern Shanghai **urban**② culture.

上海里弄,又称"弄堂",是上海最独特、最重要的居住形式。受中外建筑的影响,上海里弄与上海人的生活息息相关,体现了近代上海城市文化的特征。

There are many varieties of Lilong in Shanghai, among which Shikumen Lilong is the most famous and influential Shanghai Lilong. At present, Lilong in Shanghai is not only a place for many Shanghai people to relax and have fun, but also an important place for trade. Tianzifang, for example, is one of the most distinctive Lilong buildings in Shanghai.

上海里弄种类丰富,其中,石库门里弄是最著名和最具影响力的里弄。目前,上海里弄既是许多上海人休闲娱乐的场所,也是重要的贸易场所。比如,田子坊是上海建筑中最具特色的里弄。

Shanghai Lilong residence has a strong **spatial**③ art feature, and the residents' living space is divided into streets, general alleys, branches, and interiors in an orderly manner. This spatial organization can make residents have a strong sense of region, identity and security, and it is easy to produce a **harmonious**④ and close neighborhood relationship.

上海里弄住宅具有强烈的空间艺术特征,居民的居住空间被有序地分隔成街道、总弄、支弄和住宅内部。这种空间组织不仅能让居民产生强烈的地域感、认同感和安全感,而且容易营造出和睦亲密的邻里关系。

佳句点睛　Punchlines

1. Shanghai Lilong, also known as the "alley", is the most unique and important residential form in Shanghai, representing the characteristics of modern Shanghai urban culture.

上海里弄,又称"弄堂",是上海最独特、最重要的居住形式,体现了近代上海城市文化的特征。

2. Shanghai Lilong residence has a strong spatial art feature in the spatial arrangement, and it is rich in variety.

上海里弄住宅在空间排列上具有强烈的空间艺术特征,种类丰富多样。

3. Shanghai Lilong can make residents have a strong sense of region, identity and security, and it is easy to produce a harmonious and close neighborhood relationship.

上海里弄不仅能让居民产生强烈的地域感、认同感和安全感,容易营造出和谐亲密的邻里关系。

 生词注解　Notes

① residential /ˌrezɪˈdenʃl/　*adj.* 住宅的;与居住有关的

② urban /ˈɜːbən/　*adj.* 城市的;住在都市的

③ spatial /ˈspeɪʃl/　*adj.* 空间的;存在于空间的

④ harmonious /haːˈməʊnɪəs/　*adj.* 和谐的;和睦的

客家土楼

Hakka Tulou

导入语 Lead-in

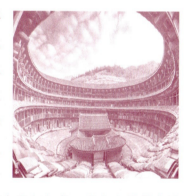

客家土楼源于宋元时期，既是客家祖先智慧的结晶，也是客家人世代相袭、聚族而居的大型群体楼房住宅，主要由福建客家土楼和广东客家土楼组成。客家土楼因规模宏大和外形独特而被誉为"东方古城堡"。客家土楼建筑是客家人继承和发扬中国传统文化的产物，与客家人的历史密切相关。客家人原是中原一带的汉民，因宋元时期的战乱和饥荒而被迫南迁到闽、粤、赣三省边区，从而形成客家民系。在背井离乡和历经磨难的过程中，客家人意识到任何困难都得依靠自己人团结互助、同心协力才能共渡难关，因此客家人总是聚居在一起，从而形成了客家人独特的建筑形式——土楼。客家土楼在造型上具有较高的审美价值，如土楼中圆

寨的造型最具艺术性和纪念性，圆形与天穹呼应，天然的黄土墙与大地紧密相连。客家土楼的厚墙是中国传统住宅内向性的极端表现，可以起到防御性作用，能让客家人获得足够的安全保障。2008年，以永定客家土楼为主体的福建土楼被列入《世界遗产名录》。

文化剪影　Cultural Outline

Hakka Tulou, made up of Fujian Hakka Tulou and Guangdong Hakka Tulou, is the **crystallization**① of the wisdom of Hakka ancestors, who were originally the Han people in the Central Plains and forced to move south due to wars and **famines**② in the Yuan and Song dynasties. Besides, Hakka Tulou, known as "Ancient Oriental Castle" because of its large scale and unique shape, has been handed down from generation to generation by the Hakka people.

客家土楼由福建客家土楼和广东客家土楼组成，是客家祖先智慧的结晶。客家祖先是来自中原的汉族人，他们因宋元时期的战乱和饥荒被迫背井离乡而南迁，被称为客家人。客家土楼因规模宏大、外形独特而被誉为"东方古城堡"，并被客家人代代相传。

Hakka Tulou was built according to China's traditional thought of Eight Diagrams holding that the heaven is round and the earth is square. For instance, Yongding Hakka Tulou includes varieties of square and round houses. In addition, Hakka Tulou has thick walls and **ingenious**③ structure, which is the product of the development of traditional Chinese culture, with various functions such as protection against high winds, earthquakes and hot and cold weather as well as a guard against enemies.

客家土楼是根据中国传统八卦理念"天圆地方"而建造的。比如,永定客家土楼包括各种方形和圆形的土楼。此外,客家土楼墙厚,结构精巧,是中国传统文化发展的产物,具有防风、抗震和冬暖夏凉的作用及抵御外敌的功能。

Hakka Tulou is of high **aesthetic**④ value in modeling with the shape of the circle corresponding to the sky and the natural **loess**⑤ wall closely connected with the earth. On top of that, there are a significant number of articles with the cultural connotation in the Tulou, such as pillar couplets, stone carvings, ancient calligraphy, and other cultural treasures, reflecting the Hakkas spirit of diligence, intelligence, **thrift**⑥, **solidarity**⑦ and **patriotism**⑧.

客家土楼造型具有很高的美学价值,圆形与天穹呼应,天然的黄土墙与大地紧密相连。此外,土楼中还有大量具有文化内涵的物品,如对联、石刻、古书法和其他文化瑰宝等,体现了客家人勤劳、智慧、节俭、团结、爱国的精神。

 佳句点睛　Punchlines

1. Hakka Tulou, known as "Ancient Oriental Castle", is the crystallization of the Hakka ancestors' wisdom.

客家土楼被誉为"东方古城堡",是客家祖先智慧的结晶。

2. Hakka Tulou was built according to the traditional Chinese thought of Eight Diagrams holding that the heaven is round and the earth is square.

客家土楼是根据中国传统八卦理念"天圆地方"而建造的。

3. Hakka Tulou retains a significant number of articles with the cultural connotation, reflecting the Hakkas' spirit of diligence, intelligence, thrift, solidarity and patriotism.

客家土楼保留了大量具有文化内涵的物品，反映了客家人勤劳、智慧、节俭、团结、爱国的精神。

 情景对话　Situational Dialogue

A: Professor Lin, I wanna write my paper on traditional Chinese residence. Can you offer me some relevant information?

B: Surely. Traditional Chinese houses are widely **distributed**[9], showcasing obvious regional characteristics and reflecting different living customs and aesthetic concepts. For example, Beijing's Siheyuan adopts the central axis symmetrical wood frame courtyard structure; Shanghai Lilong has spatial artistic characteristics that reflects the characteristics of modern Shanghai urban culture; Hakka Tulou in the western part of Fujian Province applies the circular structure of large earth buildings, and so on.

A: Terrific. I have been to Hakka Tulou, known as "Ancient Oriental Castle" built on the traditional Chinese thought of Eight Diagrams holding that the heaven is round and the earth is square.

B: Right. Hakka Tulou, made up of Fujian Hakka Tulou and Guangdong Hakka Tulou, is the crystallization of the wisdom of the Hakka ancestors. If you wanna get a deep knowledge about them, you'd better go to our school library to read some related books and papers.

A: Thank you very much. I'll go there right away.

B: My pleasure. Good luck to you.

A: 林教授,我想写一篇关于中国传统民居的论文。你能给我提供一些相关信息吗?

B: 当然可以。中国传统民居分布广泛,具有明显的地域特色,反映了不同的生活习俗和审美观念。比如,北京四合院采用中轴线对称木框架庭院结构;上海里弄具有明显的空间艺术特色,反映了现代上海城市文化特征;福建西部客家土楼是巨大的圆形结构,等等。

A: 好极了。我去过客家土楼,那里有"东方古城堡"之称,是根据中国传统八卦理念"天圆地方"而建造的。

B: 对。客家土楼由福建客家土楼和广东客家土楼组成,是客家先民智慧的结晶。如果你想进一步了解,可以去我们学校图书馆看一些相关的书籍或论文。

A: 非常感谢,我现在就去。

B: 不客气,祝你好运。

生词注解 Notes

① crystallization /ˌkrɪstəlaɪˈzeɪʃn/ *n.* 结晶化；具体化

② famine /ˈfæmɪn/ *n.* 饥荒；饥饿

③ ingenious /ɪnˈdʒiːnɪəs/ *adj.* 精巧的；有独创性的

④ aesthetic /iːsˈθetɪk/ *adj.* 美学的；审美的

⑤ loess /ˈləʊɪs/ *n.* 黄土

⑥ thrift /θrɪft/ *n.* 节俭；节约

⑦ solidarity /ˌsɒlɪˈdærətɪ/ *n.* 团结，团结一致

⑧ patriotism /ˈpeɪtrɪətɪzəm/ *n.* 爱国主义；爱国精神

⑨ distribute /dɪˌstrɪbjuːt/ *vt.* 分布；分配

第四部分 服 饰

Part Ⅳ Dress

旗袍

Cheongsam

 导入语 Lead-in

旗袍是中国女性和世界华人女性的传统服装,被誉为"中国国粹"和"女性国服"。作为中国灿烂辉煌的传统服饰的代表之一,旗袍具有独特的形式美感和文化意蕴。旗袍利用色彩和款式的变化,充分展示了东方女性的体态美和曲线美,不仅深受华人女性的喜爱,也得到了外国友人的青睐。旗袍的历史演变大致经历了满人袍服、清代旗装袍、民国旗袍、现代旗袍的发展历程,从中可以看出旗袍是中国传统文化与多民族文化不断交融的产物。作为中华文化的象征形式之一,旗袍更是族群标记和华裔身份的符号。1984年,旗袍被国务院指定为女性外交人员礼服。从1990年北京亚运会起,历

次在中国举办的奥运会、亚运会、博览会和国际会议大都选择旗袍作为礼仪服装。2011年，旗袍手工制作工艺被国务院列入《第三批国家级非物质文化遗产名录》。

文化剪影　Cultural Outline

Cheongsam① (also known as Qipao) evolved from the traditional robe of the Manchu women. For nearly a hundred years, the style of cheongsam has been changing quietly and has evolved into more colorful styles influenced by the western new dress ideas. It can be said that cheongsam is a powerful proof of multicultural **integration**②.

旗袍是由满洲妇女的传统袍服演变、发展而来的。近百年来，在西方新潮服饰观念的影响下，旗袍的样式在悄然发生着变化，演变出了更加多姿多彩的样式。可以说，旗袍是多元文化交融的有力证明。

As a representative symbol of Chinese costume culture, the restrained and noble stand-up collar, the winding **frogs**③, the elegant lines and natural arc **hem**④ of Cheongsam—display the delicacy and refinement of traditional Chinese costume.

作为中国服饰文化的标志，旗袍矜持高贵的立领、婉转曲折的盘扣、优美的曲线、自然的下摆都展示着中国传统服饰的细腻与精致。

From the **ingenious**⑤ design and the **elaborate**⑥ cutting to the decorative techniques of lacing, edging, **embedding**⑦, coiling and embroidering, the birth of a cheongsam embodies the unique charm of traditional Chinese clothing.

从巧妙的设计、精心的剪裁,再到镶、滚、嵌、盘、绣等装饰工艺,一件旗袍的诞生无不体现出中国传统服饰的独特魅力。

佳句点睛 Punchlines

1. Cheongsam has the beauty of being elegant, reserved and delicate.
旗袍具有优雅大方、含蓄细腻之美。

2. Cheongsam has become a typical symbol of Chinese women's beauty.
旗袍已经成为典型的中国女性美的象征。

3. Cheongsam embodies the spirit of China's national culture.
旗袍体现了中国民族文化的精神。

情景对话 Situational Dialogue

A: I see you wore cheongsam at yesterday's party. What's your impression on cheongsam?

B: Cheongsam is the most important traditional dress in China, which reflects the typical female beauty of China, combining the style

of traditional Chinese women's dress and evening dress, so it is suitable for such an important occasion.

A: Superb. What else do you know about cheongsam?

B: The **modified**⁸ cheongsam represents a **manifestation**⁹ of the combination of the Chinese beauty and the western beauty. We can appreciate the elegant charm of Chinese women from the beauty of form and craft.

A: After hearing your explanation, I also wanna buy a cheongsam.

B: Alright. Let's go to Wangfujing Mall sometime, where there are all kinds of cheongsams.

A: That's great. Let's go sometime.

B: OK. See you there.

A: 我昨天看见你在聚会上穿了旗袍。你对旗袍的印象如何?

B: 旗袍是中国最重要的传统服饰,体现了中国典型的女性美,也结合了中国传统女装的风格和晚礼服的风格,所以在重要的场合穿着很合适。

A: 真好,你对旗袍还有哪些了解?

B: 改良后的旗袍体现了中国与西方审美的结合。我们可以从旗袍的形体美和工艺美中感受到中国女性的优雅魅力。

A: 听了你的介绍,我也想买一件旗袍。

B: 好啊,有空咱们到王府井商场看看,那里有各种款式的旗袍。

A: 太好了!咱们改日去。

B: 好的,不见不散。

生词注解　Notes

① cheongsam /tʃɒŋˈsæm/　*n.* 旗袍

② integration /ˌɪntɪˈgreɪʃn/　*n.* 整合；一体化

③ frog /frɒg/　*n.* 装饰性盘扣

④ hem /hem/　*n.* (布等的)褶边

⑤ ingenious /ɪnˈdʒiːnɪəs/　*adj.* 灵巧的；精制的

⑥ elaborate /ɪˈlæbərət/　*adj.* 精心制作的；煞费苦心的

⑦ embed /ɪmˈbed/　*vt.* 把……牢牢地嵌入(或插入、埋入)

⑧ modified /ˈmɒdɪfaɪd/　*adj.* 稍作修改的；改进的

⑨ manifestation /ˌmænɪfeˈsteɪʃn/　*n.* 显示；表明

汉服

Hanfu

导入语 Lead-in

汉服,也称"汉衣冠""汉装""华服"等,是由"黄帝尧舜垂衣裳而天下治"演变而来的,采用纺织、蜡染、夹缬、锦绣等工艺,总体风格以清淡平易为主,讲究天人合一,体现了汉民族的独特风貌。汉服有礼服和常服之分,从形制上看,主要有"上衣下裳"制(帝王百官最隆重正式的礼服)、"深衣"制(百官和士人常服)、"襦裙"制(妇女喜爱的穿着)等类型。基本特征是交领、右衽、系带和宽袖,体现了汉民族优雅洒脱、随和包容的气度。汉服的装饰图案大多采用动物、植物和几何纹样,寓意吉祥,蕴含着深厚的文化内涵。

文化剪影 Cultural Outline

Hanfu includes clothes, headwear, hairstyle, face ornaments, shoes and **accessories**①, adopting lots of crafts, such as textile, **batik**②, **jiavalerian**③, brocade, and so on. It is an essential part of Chinese **etiquette**④, highlighting the unity of man and nature and reflecting the unique features of the Han nationality.

汉服包括衣裳、首服、发式、面饰、鞋履、配饰等，采用纺织、蜡染、夹缬和锦绣等多种工艺。汉服讲究天人合一，体现了汉民族的独特风貌，是中国礼仪的重要组成部分。

The basic features of the Hanfu are the cross collar, tying to the right and the wide sleeve, reflecting the elegant and free, easy-going and **inclusive**⑤ manner of the Han nationality.

汉服的基本特征是交领、右衽、系带和宽袖，体现了汉民族优雅洒脱、随和包容的气度。

Most of the decorative patterns of Hanfu are created from animals, plants and geometric patterns, which symbolize auspiciousness and contain profound cultural connotations, showing the spirit of Han people in pursuing the unity of man and nature, standing aloof from worldly affairs and being generous and benevolent.

汉服的装饰图案大多采用动物、植物和几何纹样，寓意吉祥，蕴

含着深厚的文化内涵,表现了汉族人民追求天人合一、与世无争和宽厚仁慈的精神。

 佳句点睛　Punchlines

1. Hanfu is an essential part of Chinese etiquette, highlighting the unity of man and nature and reflecting the unique features of the Han nationality.

汉服讲究天人合一,体现了汉民族的独特风貌,是中国礼仪的重要组成部分。

2. Chinese Han Costume's common characteristics reflecting the elegant and free, easy-going and inclusive manner of the Han nationality.

汉服的总体特点体现了汉民族优雅洒脱、随和包容的风范。

3. The decorative patterns of Hanfu implies auspiciousness and contains profound cultural connotation, embodying the Han people's the spirit of pursuing the unity of man and nature, standing aloof from worldly affairs and being generous and benevolent.

汉服纹样寓意吉祥,具有深厚的文化内涵,体现了汉族人民追求天人合一、与世无争和宽厚仁慈的精神。

情景对话　Situational Dialogue

A: Hi, Lily. Thank you for inviting me to your coming-of-age ceremony. Congratulation on your coming of age.

B: Hi, Linda, thank you. Welcome to my coming-of-age ceremony.

A: You look elegant and stylish wearing such a costume. What kind of costumes is it?

B: Oh, it is Hanfu, which is an essential part of Chinese etiquette. Wearing Hanfu is very common on the coming-of-age ceremony in China.

A: Superb. What else do you know about Hanfu?

B: Hanfu emphasizes the unity of man and nature, reflecting the elegant and free, easy-going and inclusive manner of the Han nationality. Besides, it also shows the Han people's the spirit of pursuing "unity of man and nature," standing aloof from worldly affairs and being generous and benevolent.

A: After hearing your explanation, I also wanna buy a set of Hanfu for my upcoming adult ceremony.

B: Alright. You can go to Wangfujing Mall, where there are all kinds of Hanfu.

A: That's great. Thank you.

B: Never mind. Have fun.

A: 你好,莉莉。感谢你邀请我参加你的成人礼。祝贺你长大

成人。

B: 你好,琳达,谢谢。欢迎来参加我的成人礼。

A: 你这件衣服既优雅又时髦。这是什么款式的服装?

B: 噢,这是汉服,它是中国礼仪的重要组成部分。在中国的成人礼中,穿汉服是一种非常普遍的现象。

A: 真好,你对汉服还有哪些了解?

B: 汉服讲究天人合一,体现了汉民族高雅自由、随和包容的态度。此外,它还体现了汉人追求天人合一、与世无争和宽厚仁慈的精神。

A: 听了你的介绍,我也想为我即将到来的成人礼买一套汉服。

B: 好啊,你可以去王府井商场看看,那里有各种款式的汉服。

A: 太好了!谢谢你。

B: 不要客气,玩得开心。

 生词注解 Notes

① accessory /əkˈsesərɪ/ *n.* 饰品;附件

② batik /bəˈtiːk/ *n.* 蜡染色法;用蜡染色的布

③ jiavalerian /jɪavəˈlɪərɪən/ *n.* 夹缬

④ etiquette /ˈetɪkət/ *n.* 礼仪;礼节

⑤ inclusive /ɪnˈkluːsɪv/ *adj.* 包容的;包含的

⑥ geometry /dʒɪˈɒmətrɪ/ *n.* 几何学

⑦ auspiciousness /ɔːˈspɪʃəsnəs/ *n.* 吉祥;幸运

⑧ benevolence /bəˈnevələns/ *n.* 仁慈;善行

少数民族服饰

Costumes of the Ethnic Minorities

导入语 Lead-in

少数民族的服饰文化是中国民间文化的典型代表，凝聚着少数民族的性格特点、心理特征和淳厚的民俗民风，对传播中国少数民族民俗文化起着不可替代的作用。中国少数民族主要集中在西南、西北和东北各省及自治区。中国北方地区气候寒冷，尤其是东北地区的冬季十分漫长，该地区的满族、蒙古族、朝鲜族和赫哲族等少数民族偏爱袍服；西北地区的维吾尔族、哈萨克族和柯尔克孜族等少数民族服装艳丽精致，妇女喜欢穿色彩鲜艳的连衣裙，外罩对襟背心。中国南方地区，尤其是西南地区，气候温和，傣族、苗族、布依族、黎族和彝族等少数民族妇女喜

欢款式别致、轻盈飘逸的裙子等。中国少数民族的服饰款式丰富,做工精细,色彩多样,富有浓厚的生活气息和民族特色。

文化剪影 Cultural Outline

There are fifty-five ethnic minorities in China and each one has its ethnic costumes with distinctive national characteristics. In addition, the costume culture of ethnic minorities embodies the character of ethnic minorities, playing an **irreplaceable**② role in the spread of Chinese ethnic minorities folk culture.

中国有五十五个少数民族,每个少数民族都有自己独特的民族服饰。此外,少数民族服饰文化体现了本民族的特点,为中国少数民族民俗文化的传播发挥着不可替代的作用。

The ethnic minorities in the north of China, such as Manchu, Mongolian, Korean, Hezhe, and so on, prefer robes; the ethnic minorities in the northwest, such as Uighur, Kazak, Kirgiz, and so on, have **gorgeous**④ and **exquisite**⑤ costumes, and women like to wear colorful dresses and jackets; and in the southern region especially in southwest China, women of ethnic minorities, such as Dai, Miao, Buyi, Li, Yi and other ethnic minorities, like clothes with various styles and unique designs.

中国北方地区的满族、蒙古族、朝鲜族、赫哲族等少数民族偏爱袍服;西北地区的维吾尔族、哈萨克族、柯尔克孜族等少数民族服装华丽精致,妇女喜欢穿颜色鲜艳的连衣裙,外罩对襟背心;南方特别是西南地区的傣族、苗族、布依族、黎族、彝族等少数民族妇女喜欢穿着风格多样、设计独特的服装。

China's ethnic minorities mainly live in provinces and autonomous regions in the southwest, northwest, and northeast. Therefore, their ethnic costumes have formed their own unique folk customs, with ethnic costumes have various styles, fine workmanship, rich colors, strong life atmosphere, and national characteristics. They are typical representatives of Chinese folk culture.

中国少数民族主要居住在西南、西北、东北各省及自治区。因此,少数民族服饰也形成了特有的民俗习惯,风格各异,做工精细,色彩多样,富有浓厚的生活气息和民族特色,是中国民俗文化的典型代表。

 佳句点睛 **Punchlines**

1. The costume culture of ethnic minorities embodies the characteristics of ethnic minorities and plays an irreplaceable role in the spread of Chinese ethnic folk culture.

少数民族服饰文化体现了少数民族的特点,并为中国少数民族民俗文化的传播发挥着不可替代的作用。

2. Each of ethnic minorities has formed its ethnic costumes with distinctive characteristics due to their differences in geographical environment, climate, customs, economy, culture and other aspects.

各少数民族由于地理环境、气候、风俗习惯、经济文化等方面的差异,形成了各具特色的民族服饰。

3. The costumes of ethnic minorities are the typical representative of Chinese folk culture, with various styles, fine workmanship, rich colors, strong flavor of life, and national characteristics.

少数民族服饰风格各异,做工精细,色彩多样,富有浓厚的生活气息和民族特色,是中国民俗文化的典型代表。

 情景对话 Situational Dialogue

A: Your performance was very fabulous and fascinating yesterday. Your costumes are ethnic minorities' clothes of China, aren't they?

B: You're right. They're Uyghur costumes. Uyghur is one of the ethnic minorities in the northwest, where people are generally considered to have gorgeous and exquisite costumes, and women like to wear colorful dresses and jackets.

A: What else do you know relate to the costumes of China's ethnic groups?

B: Each of ethnic minorities has formed its ethnic costumes with distinctive characteristics due to their differences in geographical environment, climate, customs, economy, culture and other aspects. For example, the ethnic minorities in the north of China prefer robes.

A: After hearing your explanation, I'm deeply impressed by the costumes of China's ethnic minorities. I expect to appreciate more of them if possible.

B: Alright. You can go to the town of international **garment**⑧, where there are all kinds of costumes of China's ethnic minorities.

A: That's great. Thank you. Let's go together sometime.

B: Okay. See you there.

A: 你昨天的表演非常精彩。你穿的是中国少数民族服饰,对吧?

B: 是的,我穿的是维吾尔族服饰。维吾尔族是中国西北少数民族之一,维吾尔族服饰通常华丽精致,当地妇女喜欢穿颜色鲜艳的连衣裙,外罩对襟背心。

A: 你对少数民族服饰还有哪些了解?

B: 各少数民族因地理环境、气候、风俗习惯、经济文化等方面的差异,形成了各具特色的民族服饰。比如,中国北方的少数民族喜欢穿长袍。

A: 听了你的介绍,我对中国少数民族的服饰印象深刻。如果可以,我期望能欣赏到更多的少数民族服饰。

B: 好啊,你可以去国际服装城看看,那里有各种款式的少数民族服饰。

A: 太好了! 谢谢! 咱们改日一起去。

B: 好的,不见不散。

生词注解　Notes

① geographical /ˌdʒi:əˈɡræfɪkl/　*adj*. 地理的;地理学的

② irreplaceable /ˌɪrɪˈpleɪsəbl/ *adj.* 不可替代的；绝无仅有的

③ dissemination /dɪˌsemɪˈneɪʃn/ *n.* 宣传；散播

④ gorgeous /ˈɡɔːdʒəs/ *adj.* 华丽的；极好的

⑤ exquisite /ɪkˈskwɪzɪt/ *adj.* 精致的；优美的

⑥ autonomous /ɔːˈtɒnəməs/ *adj.* 自治的；自主的

⑦ impressive /ɪmˈpresɪv/ *adj.* 印象深刻的；感人的

⑧ garment /ˈɡɑːmənt/ *n.* 服装（比较正式，一般指整件衣服）

第五部分 节日与节气

Part Ⅴ Festivals and Solar Terms

春节

Spring Festival

导入语　Lead-in

　　春节是中华民族最隆重的传统节日，又称"年节""新春"，俗称"过大年"。春节是一年的开端，是除旧迎新的日子，也象征着团圆兴旺、幸福美满。春节是由上古时代岁首祈年祭祀演变而来的。民间谚语说："百节年为首。"春节承载了华夏民族丰厚的文化底蕴。唐代的拜年帖、宋朝的鞭炮和明清时期的守岁、赏灯、猜谜都体现出人们对幸福美好生活的憧憬和向往。民间把农历腊月二十三日到大年三十这段时间叫作"迎春日"，也叫"扫尘日"。传说中，年是一种为人们带来霉运的动物，需要用鞭炮驱赶，于是便有了燃放鞭炮的习俗。此外，还有舞狮子、耍龙灯、演社火、游花市、逛庙会等民俗活动，直到正月十五元宵节过后，春节才算过完。春节是汉族最重要的节日，满族、蒙古族、瑶族、壮族、白族、侗族、黎族、高山族、赫哲族、哈尼族、达斡尔族等也有过春节的习俗，只是他们过节的方式更有自己的民族特色。

文化剪影　Cultural Outline

Spring Festival has a long origin, which can be **traced**① back to ancient times. From the eighth day of the twelfth lunar month to the end of the first lunar month, the time **span**② is long, the **geographical**③ span is wide, and the festival activities are in various forms. It is the most important, the grandest and the liveliest traditional festival in China.

春节的起源悠久，可以追溯到上古时代。春节从腊八持续到正月底，时间延续长、地域跨度广、节日活动形式多样，是中国最重要、最隆重、最热闹的传统节日。

Spring Festival, along with Qingming Festival, Dragon Boat Festival and Mid-Autumn Festival, has become the four major traditional festivals in China, and is a common festival for Chinese children around the world. According to statistics, nearly twenty countries and regions have designated the Chinese Spring Festival as a legal holiday for the whole or part of the cities under their **jurisdiction**④. It can be seen that the Spring Festival has become an important link of cultural exchange between China and the world.

春节与清明节、端午节、中秋节并称为中国四大传统节日，是全世界中华儿女共同的盛典。据统计，已有近二十个国家和地区把中国的春节定为整体或所辖部分城市的法定节假日。由此可见，春节已经成为联系中国和世界文化交流的重要纽带。

Spring Festival is celebrated in a variety of forms, its cultural activities rich and colorful. The more common is to watch in the New Year, paste the **couplets**⑤, give the lucky money, and so on while the Spring Festival is also a grand festival of **ethnic**⑥ minorities, such as the Mongolian's White Festival, the Uygur's Eid al-adha, and so on, which all show the great expectations of the working people for the future.

春节的庆祝形式多样，文化活动丰富多彩。比较常见的有守岁、贴对联、给压岁钱等，少数民族也有类似的盛大节日，如蒙古族的白节和维吾尔族的古尔邦节等，都表现了广大劳动人民对未来的美好期待。

佳句点睛　Punchlines

1. Spring Festival is the grandest festival in the heart of all Chinese people.

春节是全体中华儿女心中最隆重的节日。

2. Spring Festival embodies the Chinese people's **unremitting**⑦ pursuit for a happy and reunited life.

春节集中体现了中国人民对美满团圆生活的不懈追求。

3. Spring Festival has become an important link of cultural

exchange between China and the world.

春节已经成为联系中国和世界文化交流的重要纽带。

 情景对话 Situational Dialogue

A: What's in your hand? Is that a piece of **calligraphy**®?

B: Yes, my teacher wrote it for me. But it also has a special name called spring couplets. I'm gonna take it home and paste it on the door during Spring Festival.

A: That sounds good. Do you know anything about Spring Festival?

B: Yes, I do. It is a traditional festival of the Chinese nation, and also the most solemn and formal festival. On this occasion, people would cele-brate it in a variety of ways, such as eating dumplings, pasting spring couplets, and so on. I love eating dumplings.

A: You're right. Spring Festival Day is very lively. If you're free that day, welcome to my home. The dumplings I make are especially delicious.

B: Oh yeah? That's great.

A:你手里拿的什么啊？是一幅书法作品吗？

B:是的,这是我的老师写给我的。不过,它还有个特别的名字叫"春联"。我打算把它带回家,等春节时贴。

A:听起来很不错,你了解春节吗？

B: 是的。春节是中华民族的传统节日,也是最隆重、最正式的节日。每到这一天,人们都会通过各种方式庆祝,像吃饺子、贴春联等。我最爱吃饺子了。

A: 说得对,春节当天非常热闹,如果有时间,欢迎你到我家做客,我包的饺子特别好吃。

B: 噢,是吗?太好了!

生词注解　Notes

① trace /treɪs/　*vi.* 追溯;追踪

② span /spæn/　*n.* 一段时间;跨距

③ geographical /ˌdʒɪəˈɡræfɪkə/　*adj.* 地理学的;地理性的

④ jurisdiction /ˌdʒʊərɪsˈdɪkʃən/　*n.* 司法权;管辖区域

⑤ couplet /ˈkʌplət/　*n.* 对联;对句

⑥ ethnic /ˈeθnɪk/　*adj.* 种族的;人种的

⑦ unremitting /ˌʌnrɪˈmɪtɪŋ/　*adj.* 不懈的;不间断的

⑧ calligraphy /kəˈlɪɡrəfi/　*n.* 书法;书法艺术

元宵节

Lantern Festival

导入语　Lead-in

元宵节,又称"上元节""小正月""元夕""灯节",是中国的传统节日之一,以喜庆的观灯习俗为主。自汉朝时起,司马迁创建《太初历》,将元宵节定为重要节日,一直延续至今。古人称"夜"为"宵",正月十五是一年中的第一个月圆之夜,也是一元的轮回,天地回春的夜晚,隋朝时称之为"元夕"或"元夜",唐初称"上元",唐末称"元宵",到了宋朝以后则称"灯夕",清朝称"灯节"。元宵节有赏花灯、吃汤圆、猜灯谜、放烟花、耍龙灯、舞狮子、踩高跷、划旱船、扭秧歌等习俗。2008年,元宵节被国务院列入《第二批国家级非物质文化遗产名录》。

文化剪影　Cultural Outline

Lantern Festival is the **continuation**① of the celebration of the new year. From Spring Festival to Lantern Festival, people's range of activities are been gradually expanded, so are interpersonal relationships. People express their yearning and longing for the new year by enjoying beautiful lanterns, eating sweet dumplings, dancing in lion costumes, rowing land boats, and other folk activities. In 2008, Lantern Festival was included in *The Second Batch of National* **Intangible**② *Cultural Heritage*.

元宵节是新春庆贺活动的延续,从春节到元宵节,人们的活动范围逐渐扩大,人际关系也逐步扩展。人们用赏花灯、吃汤圆、舞狮子、划旱船等各式各样的民俗活动来表达对新的一年的憧憬和向往。2008年,元宵节入选《第二批国家级非物质文化遗产名录》。

Lantern Festival, along with Shangsi Festival and Qixi Festival, is known as "Eastern Valentine's Day", when unmarried men and women bound by the **feudal**③ tradition can take the opportunity and get advantage of the festival, going out of the houses, and playing with each other while they may find boyfriends or girlfriends for themselves. During this period, it is also the time for young men and women to meet their loved ones. Therefore, it can be said that Lantern Festival is the most **authentic**④ Valentine's Day.

民俗文化

元宵节与上巳节、七夕节并称为"东方情人节",元宵灯会这天,被封建传统社会束缚的未婚男女可以借着过节的机会,走出家门,结伴游玩,顺便可以为自己物色对象。在此期间,也是青年男女与心上人相会的时机。因此,元宵节可以说是最正宗的情人节了。

Lantern Festival conveys the ancient cultural gene of China. People eat "sweet dumplings (tangyuan)", which is similar to the sound of "tuanyuan", which symbolizes reunion. For the same reason, "Deng (lantern)" is the **homophone**⑤ of "Ding", which means "Man". People watch lanterns on this occasion, and have the intention of praying for **heirs**⑥.

元宵节传递着中国古老的文化基因,人们食用的"汤圆"与"团圆"字音相近,象征团团圆圆。同理,"灯"字谐音"丁",意为"人丁",人们这天观赏花灯,也有求子、祈盼人丁兴旺之意。

 佳句点睛 Punchlines

1. Lantern Festival is linked with Spring Festival and is the continuation of Spring Festival.

元宵节与春节相接,是春节的延续。

2. Lantern Festival **reposes**⑦ people's wishes for the New Year and hopes for the future.

元宵节寄托了人们对新年的祈盼和对未来的憧憬。

3. Lantern Festival is a traditional festival of the Chinese nation and a symbol of reunion.

元宵节是中华民族的传统节日,是团圆的象征。

情景对话 Situational Dialogue

A: What have you been up to lately?

B: I have been preparing for an important exam recently.

A: Good luck, but be careful to **strike**® a proper balance between work and rest.

B: Yes, I know. I'm gonna relax. Do you have any idea?

A: Ok, tomorrow is Lantern Festival, so there will be streams of people **bustling**® with activity, there will be many beautiful lanterns in the evening that we can guess lantern riddles.

B: Oh yeah? That's great. Where is it?

A: On Zhonghua Road. We can go there together.

B: OK, how about seeing you at the school gate at 6 o'clock tomorrow evening?

A: Of course. See you tomorrow.

B: See you tomorrow.

A: 你最近在忙什么啊?

B: 我在准备一场重要的考试。

A: 祝你好运,不过也要注意劳逸结合。

B: 是的,我知道,我打算放松一下,你有什么建议吗?

A: 明天是元宵节,届时将人山人海,有许多热闹的活动,晚上还会有用来猜灯谜的漂亮灯笼。

B: 噢,是吗? 太好了! 在什么地方啊?

A: 在中华路上,咱们可以一起去。

B: 好的,明天下午六点校门口见怎么样?

A: 当然可以,明天见。

B: 明天见。

生词注解　Notes

① continuation /kənˌtɪnjuˈeɪʃn/　*n.* 继续;延续

② intangible /ɪnˈtændʒəbl/　*adj.* 无形的

③ feudal /ˈfjuːdl/　*adj.* 封建制度的;领地的

④ authentic /ɔːˈθentɪk/　*adj.* 正宗的;真正的

⑤ homophone /ˈhɒməfəʊn/　*n.* 同音字;同音异义词

⑥ heir /eə(r)/　*n.* 后嗣;嗣子

⑦ repose /rɪˈpəʊz/　*vt.* 寄托于……;使……休息

⑧ strike /straɪk/　*vt.* 达到(平衡);突然想到

⑨ bustle /ˈbʌsl/　*vi.* 熙熙攘攘;喧闹

清明节

Qingming Festival

导入语 Lead-in

清明节始于周朝。《淮南子·天文训》记载:"春分后十五日,斗指乙,则清明风至。"《岁时百问》载曰:"万物生长此时,皆清洁而明净。故谓之清明。"清明前后,气温回暖,万物复苏,生机盎然,适宜春耕春种,正所谓"清明前后,点瓜种豆""植树造林,莫过清明"。同时,清明节集自然节气与人文情怀于一体,是人们祭祀祖先、缅怀先辈、慎终追远、继志述事的大好时节。清明节是传统的春祭节日,整修坟墓、供奉祭品等活动有利于弘扬孝道亲情、唤醒家族共同记忆、提高家族成员的凝聚力,形成良好有序的社会氛围。此外,踏青、插柳、放风筝等活动也必不可少,人们借此亲近自然,也体现了中国传统的天人合一的思想。

文化剪影 Cultural Outline

Qingming Festival **combines**① the essence of Cold Food Festival and Shangsi Festival and **integrates**② the customs of cold food with the activities of Shangsi spring outing, making it a special festival to remember the **ancestors**③, promote filial **piety**④, and go on a spring outing to feel nature.

清明节融合了寒食节与上巳节的精华,将寒食风俗与上巳踏青的活动融为一体,使其成为一个怀念祖先、弘扬孝道、踏青郊游、感受自然的特殊节日。

Qingming Festival embodies the traditional virtues of the Chinese nation, such as honoring their ancestors, inheriting the ancestors' legacy, adapting to the weather and following the laws of nature. In ancient China, people would hold ancestor worship activities in various ways during Qingming Festival to express their sorrows for their ancestors from emperors, generals and ministers to common people. After sweeping tombs and earthing up, they could feel the taste of spring in the outing.

清明节体现了中华民族孝敬祖先、继承祖先遗志和顺应天时、遵循自然规律的传统美德。在中国古代,上至帝王将相,下到布衣百姓,在清明节时都会以各种方式进行祭祖活动,既可表达对祖先的哀思,又可在扫墓培土之余的踏青郊游中感受春天的情趣。

During Qingming Festival, people would eat cold food, fly kites and plant willow trees to ward off evil spirits. Wuzhen and other silkworm towns would also have "Silkworm Flower Show" during the festival, which are crowded with frequent and **diverse**⑤ activities and extremely rich water-town characteristics.

清明节时,人们要吃冷食、放风筝、插柳辟邪。乌镇等蚕乡在节日期间还会举行"蚕花会",会上人山人海,活动频繁多样,极富水乡特色。

佳句点睛 Punchlines

1. Qingming Festival contains the common feelings and the blood heritage of Chinese at home and abroad.

清明节蕴含着海内外华人共同的家国情怀和血脉传承。

2. Qingming Festival is an important festival for the Chinese nation to promote filial piety culture and get close to nature.

清明节是中华民族弘扬孝道文化和亲近自然的重要节日。

3. Qingming Festival is an important opportunity to improve national **cohesion**⑥ and **centripetal**⑦ force.

清明节是提高民族凝聚力和向心力的重要契机。

情景对话 Situational Dialogue

A: Hello, Mary. I didn't expect to see you here. I'm so glad.

B: Hello, Mrs. Wang. I'm glad to meet you, too.

A: Are you busy lately? I'd like to invite you to go to my house and drink coffee tomorrow.

B: I'm sorry, but I have to attend an important meeting tomorrow.

A: Oh, that's too bad. I want you to try my new **latte**®.

B: Maybe we can change the time. What about Qingming Festival?

A: I'm going home with my husband to worship my ancestors. As you know, it is an important festival for Chinese people.

B: Really? What do they do on Qingming Festival?

A: They return to their hometown, sweep the grave for their ancestors and worship the latter.

B: All right, when you come back from hometown, we can have a cup of coffee.

A: OK, that's a deal.

B: It's a deal.

A: 你好,玛丽。没想到能在这里见到你,我太开心了。

B: 你好,王太太。见到你,我也很开心。

A: 你最近忙吗?我想请你明天到我家喝咖啡。

B: 很抱歉,明天我要参加一个重要会议。

A: 噢,那太不巧了,我本来想让你品尝一下我的新式拿铁。

B: 或许我们可以换个时间,清明节怎么样?

A: 清明节我要和丈夫回老家祭祖。你知道的,清明节对中国人来说是一个重要的节日。

B: 真的吗?中国人在清明节这天都做些什么?

A: 他们会回老家为祖先扫墓、祭拜先人。

B: 好吧,那等你回来我们再一起喝咖啡。

A: 好的,一言为定。

B: 一言为定。

生词注解 Notes

① combine /kəmˈbaɪn/ *vt.* 使……联合;使……结合

② integrate /ˈɪntɪɡreɪt/ *vt.* 使……一体化;集成

③ piety /ˈpaɪətɪ/ *n.* 虔诚;孝敬

④ ancestor /ˈænsestə(r)/ *n.* 祖先;始祖

⑤ diverse /daɪˈvɜːs/ *adj.* 多种多样的;形形色色的

⑥ cohesion /kəʊˈhiːʒn/ *n.* 凝聚力

⑦ centripetal /ˌsentrɪˈpiːtl/ *adj.* 向心的;利用向心力的

⑧ latte /ˈlɑːteɪ/ *n.* 拿铁(一种加牛奶的浓咖啡)

端午节

Dragon Boat Festival

导入语　Lead-in

端午节，又称"端阳节"和"龙舟节"。节期在农历五月初五，按干支时间便是午月午日，传说此日苍龙七宿飞升于正南中天，《周易》称之为"飞龙在天"。大量出土文物和考古研究表明，端午节由上古时代的先民创立，起初是用于祭龙、祭祖的。后世的民间传说大多记载端午节是纪念屈原的节日，这一说法影响最广、最深，已经占据了主流地位。据史料记载，早在屈原之前，端午节就已形成，很多节气习俗如赛龙舟、吃粽子等与之并无太大关系，但千百年来，屈原写下的大量诗辞和其高尚的爱国主义情怀已经深入人心。2009年，端午节被联合国教科文组织列入《人类非物质文化遗产代表作名录》。

文化剪影　Cultural Outline

Dragon Boat Festival is one of the four traditional festivals of the Chinese nation with a long history. The earliest was an **auspicious**[①] day for the ancestors of the south to worship the dragon ancestor while the north regarded the fifth day of the fifth lunar month as the "Evil Month and Day", which needed to get rid of the disease and prevent the **epidemic**[②], attaching the story of Qu Yuan, a poet of Chu. It can be said that Dragon Boat Festival is the product of the **integration**[③] of southern and northern customs, natural festivals and humane morals.

端午节源远流长，是中华民族四大传统节日之一。最早是南方先民拜祭龙祖的吉日，而北方将农历五月五日视为"恶月恶日"，需要祛除病害、防止疫疾，又附会楚国诗人屈原的事迹。可以说，端午节是南北方风俗习惯、自然节令与人文道德融合的产物。

According to the **textual**[④] research, when Qu Yuan, a poet of Chu, witnessed the capital of Chu was conquered by the Qin army, he felt as if a sword being twisted in his heart, but he was helpless. On May 5, he wrote *Yearning for Changsha*, his last masterpiece, and threw himself into the Miluo River with a great stone in his arms to commit suicide. Therefore, Dragon Boat Festival is of an additional layer of **patriotic**[⑤] connotation.

据考证，楚国诗人屈原眼见秦军攻破楚国京都，心如刀绞，却无

可奈何,五月五日写下绝笔《怀沙》,抱石投汨罗江自尽。因此,端午节又多了一层爱国主义的内涵。

Dragon Boat Festival has many customs, among which the most common are the dragon boat racing, eating zongzi, and so on. Because yangqi is **exuberant**⑥ in midsummer, there are also many contents for avoiding evil and preventing diseases, such as hanging wormwood, tying multicolored silk threads, and so on, all of which have placed people's hopes for **eliminating**⑦ diseases and disasters and yearning for a beautiful and happy life.

端午节有很多风俗,最常见的有赛龙舟、吃粽子等。因为正值仲夏时节,阳气旺盛,所以又有很多避阴邪、防病疫的内容,如挂艾草、系五彩丝线等,都寄托了人们对消病祛灾的期盼和对美好幸福生活的向往。

佳句点睛 Punchlines

1. Dragon Boat Festival is the product of the fusion of the customs of north and south of China.

端午节是中国南北方风俗习惯融合的产物。

2. The origin and development of Dragon Boat Festival is an **imperceptible**⑧ process.

端午节的起源和发展是一个潜移默化的过程。

3. Dragon Boat Festival has included rich cultural connotation and deep spiritual foundation.

端午节囊括了丰富的文化内涵和深厚的精神底蕴。

情景对话 Situational Dialogue

A: Hello, Xiaoming. How's it going?

B: Hello, David. I'm fine. What about you?

A: Not bad. A Chinese friend of mine said that Dragon Boat Festival would come soon. He gave me a model of a dragon boat. Do you know anything about Dragon Boat Festival?

B: Of course. It is a traditional festival of the Chinese nation. It is rumored to **commemorate**① Qu Yuan, a patriotic poet of the Spring and Autumn period and Warring States period.

A: That sounds meaningful. Is there anything else?

B: And we'll celebrate Dragon Boat Festival by racing dragon boats and eating zongzi. Do you like zongzi? It's very delicious.

A: Oh, I haven't tasted it yet.

B: That's a **coincidence**②. My grandma's zongzi is very delicious. You can come to my house tomorrow. We'll have Dragon Boat Festival together.

A: Really? Thank you so much. See you tomorrow.

B: Okay, see you tomorrow.

A: 你好,小明。最近怎么样?

B: 你好,大卫。我很好,你呢?

A: 还不错。我的一位中国朋友说端午节快到了,送给我一艘龙舟模型。你对端午节了解吗?

B: 当然了,端午节是中华民族的传统节日,传说是用来纪念春秋战国时期的爱国诗人屈原的。

A: 听起来很有意义,还有什么吗?

B: 我们还会用赛龙舟、吃粽子的方式庆祝端午节。你喜欢粽子吗?它美味可口。

A: 噢,我还没有品尝过。

B: 那太巧了,我奶奶包的粽子特别好吃,明天你可以来我家,我们一起过端午节。

A: 真的吗?多谢!明天见。

B: 好的,明天见。

 ## 生词注解 Notes

① auspicious /ɔːˈspɪʃəs/ *adj.* 吉祥的;吉利的

② epidemic /ˌepɪˈdemɪk/ *n.* 流行病;传染病

③ integration /ˌɪntɪˈɡreɪʃən/ *n.* 融合;一体化

④ textual /ˈtekstʃuəl/ *adj.* 文本的;篇章的

⑤ patriotic /ˌpætriˈɒtɪk/ *adj.* 爱国的;爱国精神的

⑥ exuberant /ɪɡˈzjuːbərənt/ *adj.* 生机勃勃的;繁茂的

⑦ eliminate /ɪˈlɪmɪneɪt/ vt. 消除；排除

⑧ imperceptible /ˌɪmpəˈseptəbl/ adj. 感觉不到的；极细微的

⑨ commemorate /kəˈeməreɪt/ vt. 庆祝；纪念

⑩ coincidence /kəʊˈɪnsɪdəns/ n. 巧合；一致

七夕节

Qixi Festival

导入语 Lead-in

七夕节,也称"七月七"或"乞巧节",发端于上古,发展于西汉,繁荣于宋代,由星宿崇拜演变而来,因为牛郎星与织女星所在的方位比较特殊,一年才相遇一次,因此人们观察到这一天文现象后,便创作出"牛郎织女"的美丽爱情传说。民间传说农历七月七日是天上魁星的诞辰,魁星是主宰文章兴衰的神灵,科举制度下的学子格外崇拜魁星,因此就有了拜魁星之说。"坐看牵牛织女星"是民间的传统习俗,传说在七夕的夜晚,抬头可以看到牛郎织女在银河相会,瓜果架下可以偷听到牛郎织女相会时的绵绵情话。此外,还有吃乞巧果、为牛贺生、祭拜织女、穿针乞七、晒书、晒衣服等风俗习惯。

文化剪影　Cultural Outline

Qixi Festival a **comprehensive**① traditional festival, based on the legend of "Cowherd and Weaving Girl," targeting a vast number of young men and women. It is also a representative example of Chinese ancient **astrological**② culture.

七夕节是一个以"牛郎织女"的爱情传说为基础，面向广大青年男女的综合性传统节日，也是中国古代星象文化的典型事例。

Qixi Festival is the most romantic festival in the traditional culture of the Chinese nation, a symbol of loyalty and **perseverance**③ to love, and has produced the cultural meaning of "Chinese Valentine's Day" in contemporary times. In 2006, Qixi Festival was included in *The First Batch of National* **Intangible**④ *Cultural* **Heritage**⑤ *List.*

七夕节是中华民族传统文化中最具有浪漫主义色彩的节日，是对爱情忠诚和坚守的象征，并在当代产生了"中国情人节"的文化含义。2006年，七夕节被列入《第一批国家级非物质文化遗产名录》。

Qixi Festival is Double Seventh Festival to celebrate the annual reunion of lovers. Since the ancient times, there have been many ways to celebrate Qixi Festival among the Chinese people, especially in southern Fujian and Zhejiang, where people set up incense tables, offering sacrifices to the distant stars, and on the incense tables there will be

a variety of **ingenious**⁶ toys, flowers and fruits prepared by young women in advance, and then go through a series of complex links to finally complete the whole ceremony.

七夕节是女子乞巧的日子。自古以来，中国民间都有很多庆祝方式，特别是闽南、浙江一带，七夕节当天傍晚，人们摆设香案，遥祭星宿，香案上会有青年女子提前备好的各种乞巧的玩具和鲜花水果等，经过一系列复杂环节，最终完成整个仪式。

 佳句点睛　Punchlines

1. Qixi Festival is Chinese's Valentine's Day, full of romantic atmosphere.

七夕节是中国式情人节，极富浪漫主义气息。

2. Qixi Festival shows women's pursuit of **deft**⁷ knitting techniques and a happy marriage.

七夕节表现了女子对娴熟针织技法和美满婚姻的追求。

3. Qixi Festival is a major **breakthrough**⁸ in feudal **ethics**⁹ for young men and women.

七夕节是青年男女对封建礼教的重大突破。

情景对话　Situational Dialogue

A: Hi, Tom.

B: Hi, Xiaowei.

A: I have some good news for you. My elder brother will get married next week. The wedding day happens to be Qixi Festival.

B: Really? Best wishes to him! Why hold a wedding on Qixi Festival?

A: Do you know about Qixi Festival? It's Chinese Valentine's Day. It is said that getting married on Qixi Festival will be blessed by fairies.

B: Oh, **Gosh**①! That's so romantic!

A: If it's okay with you, I'd like you to be my best man. Are you free?

B: Of course, it's my honor.

A: 嗨,汤姆。好久不见!

B: 你好,小伟。好久不见!

A: 我有一个好消息要告诉你,我的哥哥下周就要结婚了,婚礼当天正好是七夕节。

B: 真的吗? 由衷地祝福他! 为什么要在七夕节举办婚礼呢?

A: 你知道七夕节吗? 这是中国的情人节,传说在七夕节结婚会得到仙女的祝福。

B: 噢,天哪! 真的太浪漫了!

民俗文化

A: 如果方便的话,我想邀请你去做伴郎。你有时间吗?
B: 当然有,这是我的荣幸。

生词注解 Notes

① comprehensive /ˌkɒmprɪˈhensɪv/ *adj.* 综合性的;广泛的

② astrological /ˌæstrəˈlɒdʒɪkl/ *adj.* 星象的;占星术的

③ perseverance /ˌpɜːsəˈvɪərəns/ *n.* 坚持不懈;坚定不移

④ intangible /ɪnˈtændʒəbl/ *adj.* 无形的

⑤ heritage /ˈherɪtɪdʒ/ *n.* 遗产;传统

⑥ ingenious /ɪnˈdʒiːnɪəs/ *adj.* 灵巧的;精制的

⑦ deft /deft/ *adj.* 灵巧的;敏捷熟练的

⑧ breakthrough /ˈbreɪkθruː/ *n.* 突破;突破性进展

⑨ ethics /ˈeθɪks/ *n.* 伦理学;行为准则

⑩ gosh /ɡɒʃ/ *int.* (非正式,表惊讶)天哪;上帝

中秋节

Mid-Autumn Festival

导入语　Lead-in

中秋节,又称"月夕""月亮节""秋节""仲秋节""八月节""八月会""拜月节""团圆节"等。中秋节与端午节、春节、清明节并称为"中国四大传统节日"。中秋节最早起源于上古时期的天象崇拜,有祭月、赏月、拜月、吃月饼、赏桂花、饮桂花酒等习俗。迄今,过中秋节依然是全体中华儿女难以割舍的民族情怀。中秋节在农历八月十五,八月是秋季的第二月,故称"仲秋"。中秋月圆人团圆,中秋节已经成为中国各族人民及世界华夏文化圈全体成员表达乡思乡愁、期盼团圆幸福和粮食丰收的心灵寄托。2006年,国务院将中秋节列入《第一批国家级非物质文化遗产名录》。从2008年起,中秋节被列为中国国家法定节假日。

 文化剪影 Cultural Outline

Mid-Autumn Festival has a long history and a wide influence among the people. On this day, the family get together and talk about family customs. Even the women who return to their mother's homes will go back to their husbands' homes on the occasion to **symbolize**① reunion and **auspiciousness**②. It can be said that Mid-Autumn Festival is an important opportunity for the modern society to **enhance**③ the sense of **well-being**④ and belonging of the whole people.

中秋节历史悠久,在民间影响深远。每到这一天,阖家团聚,共话家常,即使归宁的妇人该日也要返回夫家,象征团圆和吉祥。可以说,中秋节是现代社会提高全民幸福感、归属感的重要契机。

Mid-Autumn Festival is to associate the natural phenomena with human emotions, **reposing**⑤ homesickness and longing for loved ones with the full moon. And because its festival is in autumn, it has become a festival that prays for smooth weather and **bumper**⑥ harvest.

中秋节是将自然现象和人类情感联系在一起,以圆月寄托思念故乡、思念亲人之情。又因为节期在秋天,所以也就成了祈求风调雨顺和粮食丰收的节日。

Since ancient times, Mid-Autumn Festival has had the custom of eating mooncakes, drinking wine made with **osmanthus**⑦ flowers, enjoying the moon and guessing riddles. Ethnic minorities and other countries in the world also have the habit of celebrating the Mid-Autumn Festival. For example, Mongolians have the legend of "chasing the moon". On the night of Mid-Autumn Festival, people mounted their steeds and galloped in the moonlight across the prairies till the moon sets down. It can be said that Mid-Autumn Festival is a common one for all the Chinese people in the world.

中秋节自古就有吃月饼、饮桂花酒、赏月、猜谜的风俗，中国少数民族和世界其他国家也有欢度中秋的习惯。如蒙古族有"追月"之说，在中秋之夜，人们跨上骏马，在月色之中的草原上奔驰，直到月亮西下。中秋节可以说是世界全体中华儿女共同的节日。

 佳句点睛　**Punchlines**

1. Mid-Autumn Festival is a day of family reunion and celebrating the harvest and the essence of agricultural civilization.

中秋节是阖家团圆、庆祝丰收的日子，是农耕文明的精华。

2. Mid-Autumn Festival is the carrier for the Chinese people to place their homesickness and **cherish**⑧ the memory of their loved ones.

中秋节是中华儿女寄托乡思、怀念亲人的载体。

3. Mid-Autumn Festival is the **epitome**⑨ of traditional Chinese culture.

中秋节是中华民族传统文化的缩影。

 情景对话 Situational Dialogue

A: Hello, Ms. Zhang. Nice to meet you!

B: Hello, Mary. Nice to meet you, too!

A: I heard that you just came to China. Do you still fit in?

B: Everything is going well. My teachers and classmates are very friendly. But they are all going home on Mid-Autumn Festival.

A: Yes, Mid-Autumn Festival is a time for family reunion. How are you gonna spend it?

B: I may be in the dorm or go out, I'm not sure yet.

A: That would be boring. I'd like to invite you to my house? My house will be very busy. My husband is a good cook.

B: I think that will **inconvenience**⑩ you.

A: It's okay, honey. We all welcome you.

B: Thank you so much.

A: OK, it's a deal. See you tomorrow.

B: See you tomorrow.

A: 你好,张女士。很高兴见到你!

B: 你好,玛丽。我也很高兴!

A: 我听说你刚到中国,还适应吗?

B: 一切都很顺利,我的老师和同学们都很友好。不过,他们中秋节都要回家了。

A：是的，中秋节是阖家团圆的日子，你打算怎么过？

B：我可能会在宿舍学习或出去玩，还没确定。

A：那太无聊了，我想邀请你到我家去。我家会非常热闹，我丈夫做得一手好菜。

B：那会给你添麻烦的。

A：没事，亲爱的，我们都很欢迎你。

B：真的太感谢你了。

A：好的，一言为定。明天见。

B：明天见。

生词注解 Notes

① symbolize /ˈsɪmbəlaɪz/　vt. 象征；用符号表现

② auspiciousness /ɔːˈspɪʃəsnəs/　n. 吉祥；吉兆

③ enhance /ɪnˈhɑːns/　vt. 提高；加强

④ well-being /ˈwel biːɪŋ/　n. 幸福；康乐

⑤ repose /rɪˈpəʊz/　vt. 寄托于……；使……休息

⑥ bumper /ˈbʌmpə/　adj. 丰盛的；巨大的

⑦ osmanthus /ɒzˈmænθəs/　n. 桂花

⑧ cherish /ˈtʃerɪʃ/　vt. 珍爱

⑨ epitome /ɪˈpɪtəmɪ/　n. 缩影；摘要

⑩ inconvenience /ˌɪnkənˈviːnɪəns/　vt. 麻烦；打扰

重阳节

Double Ninth Festival

九月初九重阳节,"九"数在古籍中是阳数,月和日均逢阳数,日月并阳,两九相重,故称"重阳",而且"九九"与"久久"同音,有天长地久、健康长寿之意。古人认为九九重阳是吉祥日子,所以重阳节还有饮宴祈寿之俗。古时候,民间会在重阳节这天登高望远、赏菊祈福、吃重阳糕、饮菊花酒、插戴茱萸。重阳节的起源可追溯到上古时代,随着历史发展演变,如今文化内涵得到了进一步拓展,也寄托了人们对老年人健康长寿的期盼。1989年,农历九月九日被定为"老人节",倡导全社会树立尊老、敬老、爱老、助老的良好风气。2006年,重阳节被国务院列入《第一批国家级非物质文化遗产名录》。

文化剪影 Cultural Outline

Double Ninth Festival is a traditional one of the Han nationality, which **integrates**① many kinds of folk customs. At first, Double Ninth Festival was a time for people to hold a harvest festival to offer sacrifices to heaven and ancestors, thank the Heaven and remember the ancestors' virtues. Then, after a series of **inheritance**② and development, there are not only the meanings of climbing high and looking far, drinking **chrysanthemum**③ wine to ward off evil spirits, and so on, but also the moral of praying for a long life for the elderly and loving them.

重阳节是融合多种民俗为一体的汉族传统节日。起初，重阳节是人们庆祝丰收、祭天祭祖、感谢上苍、感念祖德的日子，而后经过一系列的传承和发展，既有登高远眺、饮菊花酒辟邪等含义，也有为老人祈求长寿的敬老、爱老的寓意。

Double Ninth Festival is an important way for the Han ancestors to worship nature, get close to nature and **honor**④ the elders and carry forward the culture of filial piety. Mountaineering can make people feel comfortable and savor the **infinite**⑤ charm of nature; the filial piety and respect for relatives is the traditional virtue of the Chinese nation. Double Ninth Festival is the **combination**⑥ of the two, and people have a special feeling for the festival.

重阳节是汉族先民崇拜自然、亲近自然和孝敬长辈、弘扬孝道文

化的重要途径。登山望远,可使人心情舒畅,感受大自然的无穷魅力;孝老敬亲是中华民族的传统美德。重阳节集二者为一体,人们对这个节日有着非同寻常的感情。

Double Ninth Festival is in the mid-autumn season, when the sky is clear and the air is **crisp**⑦, so it is the ideal time for people and their families to travel and enjoy the scenery. Dogwood has the effect of **dispelling**⑧ insects and dampness. People are used to wearing dogwood to ward off evil and pray for good fortune.

重阳节恰逢仲秋时节,秋高气爽,正是人们和家人出游赏景的绝佳时机。茱萸具有驱虫祛湿的功效,人们习惯佩戴茱萸来辟邪求吉。

 佳句点睛　**Punchlines**

1. Double Ninth Festival is an important way for people to climb mountains enjoy chrysanthemums and get close to nature.

重阳节是人们登高赏菊、亲近自然的重要途径。

2. Double Ninth Festival has the special significance of carrying forward the culture of **filial**⑨ **piety**⑩ and leading the social fashion of respecting and loving the elderly.

重阳节具有弘扬孝道文化、引领敬老爱老社会风尚的特殊意义。

3. The main themes of Double Ninth Festival are to climb moun-

tains to enjoy the autumn and honor the elderly.

登高赏秋和感恩敬老是重阳节的两大主题。

 情景对话 Situational Dialogue

A: What have you been up to lately? I heard you went to the old folks' home.

B: Yes, that's right. I took part in Double Ninth Festival activities organized by our school and went to the old folks' home to visit the old people there.

A: You're so loving. What did you do there?

B: I sang an English song for the old people and performed a short sketch with my classmates. The old people there are very happy.

A: Oh, that sounds really meaningful.

B: Yes, it's great! If you wanna go, you can come with us next time.

A: Really? It's a deal.

B: OK, it's a deal.

A: 你最近在忙些什么啊？我听说你去了敬老院。

B: 是的，没错。我参加了学校组织的重阳节活动，去敬老院看望那里的老人们。

A: 真是太有爱心了，你在那里都做了什么？

B: 我为老人们唱了一首英文歌，还和其他同学共同表演了一个小品，老人们都很开心。

A: 噢，听起来真的太有意义了。

B: 是的，非常棒！你如果想去的话，下次可以跟我们一起。

A: 真的吗？一言为定。

B: 好的，一言为定。

生词注解　Notes

① integrate /ˈɪntɪɡreɪt/　vt. 使……一体化；整合

② inheritance /ɪnˈherɪtəns/　n. 继承；遗传

③ chrysanthemum /krɪˈzænθəməm/　n. 菊花

④ honor /ˈɒnə(r)/　vt. 尊敬；给……以荣誉

⑤ infinite /ˈɪnfɪnət/　adj. 无限的；无穷的

⑥ combination /ˌkɒmbɪˈneɪʃn/　n. 结合；组合

⑦ crisp /krɪsp/　adj. 清爽的；新鲜的

⑧ dispel /dɪˈspel/　vt. 驱散；消除

⑨ filial /ˈfɪliəl/　adj. 孝顺的；子女的

⑩ piety /ˈpaɪəti/　n. 孝敬；虔诚

二十四节气

Twenty-Four Solar Terms

 导入语 Lead-in

二十四节气是中国古代劳动人民总结出来用于指导农事活动规律的，包括立春、雨水、惊蛰、春分、清明、谷雨、立夏、小满、芒种、夏至、小暑、大暑、立秋、处暑、白露、秋分、寒露、霜降、立冬、小雪、大雪、冬至、小寒和大寒。二十四节气歌更有趣、更好记：立春雨水渐，惊蛰虫不眠，春分近清明，采茶谷雨前；立夏小满足，芒种大开镰，夏至才小暑，大暑三伏天；立秋处暑去，白露南飞雁，秋分寒露至，霜降红叶染；立冬小雪飘，大雪兆丰年，冬至数九日，小寒又大寒。2006年，二十四节气被国务院列入《第一批国家级非物质文化遗产名录》。2016年，二十四节气被联合国教科文组织列入《人类非物质文化遗产代表作名录》。

 文化剪影　Cultural Outline

Twenty-Four Solar Terms **originated**① in China's Yellow River Basin. Since ancient times, most of China's political, economic and cultural centers have been **concentrated**② in this area. Therefore, Twenty-Four Solar Terms are based on the climate and agricultural activities of the Yellow River Basin.

二十四节气起源于中国的黄河流域一带，自古以来，中国的政治经济文化中心大多集中在这一地区，因此二十四节气是以黄河流域的气候和农业活动为基础建立的。

Twenty-Four Solar Terms are an important part of the long history and culture of the Chinese nation and the **crystallization**③ of the wisdom of ancient ancestors in **exploring**④ nature, playing an important role in guiding the ancients' diet, agricultural production, and other aspects.

二十四节气是中华民族悠久历史文化的重要组成部分，是古代先民探索自然的智慧结晶，对古人的饮食起居、农业生产等方面起到了重要的指导作用。

Twenty-Four Solar Terms are the basic contents of the heavenly stems and earthly branches, reflecting the annual movement of the sun. When the sun shines directly on the Tropic of Cancer, it is the Summer **Solstice**⑤, while directly on the **Tropic of Capricorn**⁶, it is the Winter Solstice.

二十四节气是干支历法的基本内容,反映了太阳的周年运动。太阳直射北回归线为天文学上的夏至,直射南回归线则为冬至。

佳句点睛 Punchlines

1. Twenty-Four Solar Terms express the unique concept of time between man and nature.

二十四节气表达了人与自然之间独特的时间概念。

2. Twenty-Four Solar Terms contain the rich cultural connotation and historical **accumulation**⁷ of the Chinese nation.

二十四节气蕴含了中华民族丰富的文化内涵和历史积淀。

3. Twenty-Four Solar Terms are the regular system of human cognition of **phenology**⁸ and climate change in a year.

二十四节气是人类认知一年中物候和气候变化的规律体系。

情景对话 Situational Dialogue

A: Hello, Mr. Zhang. Excuse me, are you busy right now?

B: Hello, Jerry. Is anything wrong?

A: I need your help, sir. I have a problem.

B: What's wrong with you?

A: My friend asked me about Twenty-Four Solar Terms, but I knew nothing about it.

B: It's all right. Don't worry. Let me tell you. Twenty-Four Solar Terms are the natural laws of climate discovered by the ancients in China. It is a great creation, known as "The Fifth Largest Invention in China".

A: Could you tell me more about it? I feel a little **abstract**⑨.

B: Er, for example, the coming Beginning of Summer is one of the solar terms, telling people that summer is coming. If you wanna know more, we can go to the library tomorrow to discuss about it.

A: Really? That would be great! Thank you very much. See you tomorrow.

B: OK, it's all right. See you tomorrow.

A: 你好,张先生。请问你现在忙吗?
B: 你好,杰里。有什么问题吗?
A: 我遇到了一个难题,需要你的帮助。
B: 怎么了?
A: 我的朋友问我二十四节气,可我对此一无所知。
B: 没关系,别担心,我来告诉你。二十四节气是中国古人发现的关于气候的自然规律,这是一项伟大的创造,被誉为"中国第五大发明"。
A: 能说具体点吗? 我觉得有些抽象。
B: 呃,比如即将到来的立夏,就是一个节气,它告诉人们夏天就要到了。如果你想深入了解的话,我们可以明天去图书馆讨论一下。

A: 真的吗？太好了！谢谢你,明天见。

B: 好的,没关系,明天见。

生词注解 Notes

① originate /əˈrɪdʒɪneɪt/　*vi.* 发源

② concentrate /ˈkɒnsntreɪt/　*vt.* 集中；浓缩

③ crystallization /ˌkrɪstəlaɪˈzeɪʃn/　*n.* 结晶化；具体化

④ exploration /ˌekspləˈreɪʃn/　*n.* 探测；探究

⑤ solstice /ˈsɒlstɪs/　*n.* 至日；至点

⑥ Tropic of Capricorn 南回归线

⑦ accumulation /əˌkjuːmjəˈleɪʃn/　*n.* 积累；积聚

⑧ phenology /fəˈnɒlədʒɪ/　*n.* 生物气候学；物候学

⑨ abstract /ˈæbstrækt/　*adj.* 纯理论的；抽象的

第六部分 技 艺

Part Ⅵ Skills

第六部分 技艺

中医

Traditional Chinese Medicine

导入语 Lead-in

中医，又称"岐黄之术"。"岐黄"是指岐伯和黄帝。相传，公元前26至前22世纪，黄帝与他的臣子岐伯以问答形式讨论医学，并使专人记录而成中国现存最早的中医理论专著《黄帝内经》。目前学术界将《黄帝内经》与《难经》《伤寒杂病论》《神农本草经》看成是中医四大经典著作。自远古时期产生，到春秋战国时形成基本理论，历经千年实践和发展，中医形成了"望、闻、问、切"四诊法，辨清病理，对症下药；在理论上建立了"阴阳五行学说""脉象学说""经络学说"等；在疗法上使用中药、针灸、拔罐等，使机体恢复健康。2018年，中医被世界卫生组织纳入《全球医学纲要》。

文化剪影 Cultural Outline

Traditional Chinese medicine, which originated from China's primitive society, is a **comprehensive**① subject to study the human **physiology**②, **pathology**③ and the diseases diagnosis and prevention, holding that the human body is a unified organic whole composed of qi, shape and spirit, and various tissues and organs have different functions, coordinate and interacts with each other.

中医源于中国原始社会,是研究人类机体生理、病理和疾病的诊断与防治的一门综合型学科。中医认为人体是一个由气、形、神组成的统一有机整体,各个组织和器官分别具有不同的功能,相互协调,相互作用。

Traditional Chinese medicine has been developing vigorously in China for thousands of years. It plays an **irreplaceable**④ role in treatment, prevention, healthcare and preservation, and contains the feelings of the Chinese nation to help the world and save the people.

中医在中华大地上已经蓬勃发展了数千年之久,无论是在治病、预防、还是在养生、保健等方面,都发挥着不可替代的作用,蕴含了中华民族济世救人、胸怀天下的情怀。

The theoretical system of traditional Chinese medicine has been formed through long clinical practice, whose two basic characteristics are the concept of the whole and the treatment based on syndrome **differentiation**⑤. The overall concept means that the human body itself is an organic whole, which is unified with the natural environment while changes in the natural world directly or indirectly affect the operation of the body; treatment based on **syndrome**⑥ differentiation refers to the comprehensive and profound judgment of pathology and the determination of treatment methods through "The Four Diagnostic Methods".

中医的理论体系是经过漫长的临床实践形成的，整体观念和辨证论治是它的两个基本特点。整体观念是指人体本身是一个有机整体，与自然环境具有统一性，自然界的变化直接或间接地影响着机体的运行；辨证论治是指通过"四诊法"全面深刻地判断病理进而确定治疗方法。

 佳句点睛　**Punchlines**

1. Traditional Chinese medicine carries the valuable experience and theoretical knowledge of the ancient Chinese working people in the struggle against diseases, which is a strong proof of their courage to explore and **indomitable**⑦ spirit.

中医承载了中国古代劳动人民同疾病做斗争的宝贵经验和理论知识，是其勇于探索和顽强不息精神的有力证明。

2. From primitive society to modern times, traditional Chinese

medicine has maintained its unfailing vitality.

从原始社会到近现代，中医一直保持着经久不衰的生命力。

3. The theoretical system of traditional Chinese medicine originates from practice and in turn guides practice.

中医的理论体系来源于实践，又反过来指导实践。

 情景对话　Situational Dialogue

A: Hello, Mr. Wang, long time no see.

B: Hello Tom, long time no see. I didn't really expect to meet you in this old street.

A: I like this street very much, quiet, profound and antique, with an extraordinary charm.

B: Sounds wonderful! What do you say we take a look around?

A: It's a great pleasure! Mr. Wang, I seem to smell a strange aroma.

B: Oh, you're talking about the aroma of herbs in this Chinese medicine store.

A: It is the very place that sells traditional Chinese medicine. What's the meaning of the plaque on the shop "Xuan Hu Ji Shi"?

B: Let me tell you. It is said that in ancient times, there was a **plague**[①] in the Central Plains, there was no medicine to cure it. Later, an old man opened a medicine shop, where anyone who came to seek medical treatment would get medicine from a gourd, which could get rid of the disease. The plague was then soon **contained**⑨. After that the doctors always hang a gourd in front of the door. This is the story of "Xuan Hu Ji Shi (practise medicine to help the people)".

A: Sounds really amusing. Thank you.

B: My pleasure.

A: 你好,王先生,好久不见。

B: 你好,汤姆,好久不见。真没想到竟然会在这条古街上遇见你。

A: 我非常喜欢这条街,它幽静深远,古色古香,具有非凡的魅力。

B: 听上去真不错,我们一起到处转转怎么样?

A: 不胜荣幸！王先生,我好像闻到了一股奇特的香气！

B: 噢,你说的是这家中药店的草药香气吧。

A: 原来这就是卖中药的地方啊。店铺上的牌匾"悬壶济世"是什么意思啊?

B: 让我来告诉你,传说古时候中原地区发生瘟疫,无药可医,后来有一位老人开了家药铺,凡是来求医的人都会得到一只里面装着药的葫芦,并且药到病除,瘟疫很快就被遏制住了。之后,行医的人会在门前悬挂一只葫芦。这就是"悬壶济世"的故事。

A: 听起来真有趣,谢谢你。

B: 不用客气。

生词注解　Notes

① comprehensive /ˌkɒmprɪˈhensɪv/　*adj.* 全面的；综合的

② physiology /ˌfɪziˈɒlədʒi/　*n.* 生理学；生理机能

③ pathology /pəˈθɒlədʒi/　*n.* 病理学；病状

④ irreplaceable /ˌɪrɪˈpleɪsəbl/　*adj.* （因贵重或独特）不能替代的；独一无二的

⑤ differentiation /ˌdɪfəˌrenʃiˈeɪʃn/　*n.* 分化；变异

⑥ syndrome /ˈsɪndrəʊm/　*n.* 综合症状；综合征

⑦ indomitable /ɪnˈdɒmɪtəbl/　*adj.* 不屈不挠的；坚强不屈的

⑧ plague /pleɪɡ/　*n.* 瘟疫；灾祸

⑨ contain /kənˈteɪn/　*vt.* 控制；牵制

茶艺

Tea Ceremony

导入语 Lead-in

"茶"字由草、人、木组成,寓意"人在草木之间",得自然滋养而成万物灵长。上自达官贵人,下至平民百姓,品茗饮茶的习惯早已铭刻在每个中国人的骨子里。

随之产生的茶艺是一门包含选择茶叶、水源、环境和展示烹茶技术及茶具文化的行为艺术。茶艺萌生于唐代,发展于宋朝,清代时达到鼎盛。中国茶艺分为表演型茶艺、待客型茶艺、营销型茶艺和养生型茶艺。其中表演型茶艺是指茶艺师为众人表演烹茶技巧,既注重视觉效果,也注重听觉享受,以吸引大众注意力,进而传播茶文化;养生型茶艺分为传统养生茶艺和现代养生茶艺,传统养生茶艺结合了道教、佛教的打坐、入静,提倡以茶养身、以道养心。2008年,茶艺被国务院列入《第二批国家级非物质文化遗产名录》。

 文化剪影 Cultural Outline

Tea Ceremony is a kind of art which includes the judgment of tea quality, the artistic appreciation of tea cooking techniques and the enjoyment of the tea **environment**①. The series of steps involved in the tea art show embodies the unity of form and spirit. Since the Tang Dynasty, tea culture has quietly **integrated**② into the blood of the Chinese nation.

茶艺是包括茶叶优次评判、烹茶操作技术的艺术鉴赏和享受品茶环境的一门艺术。茶艺表演包含的一系列步骤体现了形式与精神的统一。从唐朝时起,茶文化已经悄无声息地融入华夏民族的血脉之中。

Kung fu Tea is an important part of tea performances. The method of making Kung fu Tea is very particular, and it takes a lot of time and effort to operate. Sipping Kung fu Tea is one of the important customs in the Chaoshan area of China, where almost every household is equipped with Kung fu Tea set.

工夫茶是茶艺表演的重要组成部分,其泡茶方法十分讲究,操作起来需要耗费大量的时间和精力。品工夫茶是中国潮汕地区重要的风俗之一,几乎家家户户都配备工夫茶具。

The performance of tea art shows an active lifestyle. The quiet and elegant environment and the close cooperation with the tea artists bring the tea drinkers noble and beautiful enjoyment and **purify**③ their souls.

茶艺表演体现了一种积极的生活方式,幽静雅致的环境与茶艺师的密切配合给饮茶者以高尚、美好的享受,使其心灵得以净化。

佳句点睛　Punchlines

1. Tea Ceremony is the daily habit of drinking tea through the art of processing, **endowing**④ tea with beauty and spirit, and then improve people's taste in life.

茶艺是指把日常饮茶的习惯通过艺术性的加工,赋茶以美感和灵性,进而提高人们的生活品味。

2. Tea Ceremony is a unique Chinese tea culture formed on the basis of the traditional Chinese culture and widely used for reference and absorbing the essence of literature and **aesthetics**⑤.

茶艺是在中华民族传统文化的基础上广泛借鉴和吸纳文学、美学等领域的精华而形成的独具特色的中国茶文化。

3. Since ancient times, the Chinese nation has been a country of civilization and **etiquette**⑥, and the rules of Tea Ceremony embody the national spirit of extending oneself to others and mutual respect and love. By cooking and tasting tea, we pursue inner peace, understand life

and explore the meaning of life.

华夏民族自古以来就是文明礼仪之邦,茶艺的规则正是体现了推己及人、互敬互爱的民族精神。通过烹茶和品茶,追求内心的平静,体悟人生,探寻生命的意义。

情景对话 Situational Dialogue

A: Hi! I haven't seen you for about three months. What have you been up to lately?

B: Hi! I've recently attended a **seminar**⑦ about traditional Chinese culture, which is specially offered for foreign students like us.

A: That sounds good! What kind of knowledge does the seminar talk about?

B: There're many aspects of this training class, such as calligraphy, traditional Chinese painting, wushu, and so on, but I'm most interested in Tea Ceremony, because I like drinking tea very much. Do you know about Tea Ceremony?

A: I know it is the rules of tea drinking through artistic transformation, in a quiet and elegant environment to give people the enjoyment of beauty, and I heard that the people performing tea are graceful.

B: You're right. Our teacher is like a graceful angel!

A: And I've heard that there're many specific names in tea art, for example, "the black dragon entering the palace" means that the Oolong Tea is put the dark-red **enameled**⑧ pottery. There're a lot of similar statements. Can you understand?

B: Some are understood but others not, but I feel that you know a lot about tea. Would you like to join this seminar with me?

A: Of course, but I'm sorry I have a very important exam recently. I'm afraid I don't have time.

B: What a pity!

A: 你好！我大概有三个月没见到你了，最近在忙什么？

B: 你好！我最近参加了一个中国传统文化研修班，是专门针对我们这样的外国留学生开设的。

A: 听起来不错！都讲些什么知识啊？

B: 这个培训班的内容有很多，像书法、国画、武术等，不过我最感兴趣的是茶艺，因为我很喜欢喝茶，你知道茶艺吗？

A: 我知道茶艺是通过把饮茶的规则进行艺术加工，在安静优雅的环境中给人以美的享受，而且我听说表演茶艺的人都很有气质。

B: 你说得对。我们的老师就像是一位优雅的天使！

A: 而且我听说茶艺中有很多特定的称呼，像"乌龙入宫"的意思就是把乌龙茶倒入紫砂壶中，还有很多类似的说法，你能明白吗？

B: 有些能，有些不能，不过我觉得你对茶艺颇有见解，你愿意和我一起参加这个研修班吗？

A: 当然愿意，不过我最近有一个非常重要的考试，恐怕没有时间。

B: 那真是太遗憾了！

 生词注解　Notes

① environment /ɪnˈvaɪrənmənt/　*n.* 环境；外界

② integrate /ˈɪntɪɡreɪt/　*v.* 成为一体

③ purify /ˈpjʊərɪfaɪ/　*vt.* 净化；使……纯净

④ endow /ɪnˈdaʊ/　*vt.* 赋予；天生具有

⑤ aesthetics /iːsˈθetɪk/　*n.* 美学；审美观

⑥ etiquette /ˈetɪkət/　*n.* 礼节；礼仪

⑦ seminar /ˈsemɪnɑː(r)/　*n.* 研讨会

⑧ enameled /ɪˈnæmld/　*adj.* 搪瓷的；上釉的

第六部分 技艺

武术

Wushu

导入语 Lead-in

武术,又称"中国功夫",与中医、京剧、书法并称为"中国四大国粹",是中国广大劳动人民长期以来在日常生活中融合兵学、中医学、气功、拳击美学等而形成的一种独特文化体系。它既包括形体上的手、眼、身、法、步,又涵盖内在的精、气、神,通过对外在体魄的锻炼以修炼身心,使修炼者内外兼修,成就"尚武崇德"的道德信念。近代以来,为了适应时代潮流,武术进行了改革和创新,成为体育范畴的重要组成部分。"把武术推向世界"是一代代中国武术人的宏伟目标。太极拳是武术的一种,2006年,太极拳被列入《第一批国家级非物质文化遗产名录》。2020年,太极拳被联合国教科文组织列入《世界非物质文化遗产名录》。2020年,武术被列入第四届青

年奥林匹克运动会正式比赛项目,这是武术首次成为奥林匹克系列运动会的正式比赛项目。

文化剪影 Cultural Outline

Wushu originated from the hunting-oriented production activities of the **ancestors**① in ancient times. In order to hunt and defend animals, people gradually **accumulated**② low-level skills such as **lopping**③ and stabbing. With the continuous progress of society, these skills have been promoted and **summarized**④, evolved into Wushu techniques, passed on and carried forward. From the Shang and Zhou dynasties, Wushu has not only been used in wars. In the peaceful era, some techniques have been artistically processed to form Wushu dances, which are of great **aesthetic**⑤ value.

武术起源于远古时期先民们以狩猎为主的生产活动。为了捕猎和防御动物,人们逐渐积累了砍、刺等低级技能。随着社会的不断进步,这些技能得到了提升和总结,演化成了武术技法并得以传承和发扬。自商周朝起,武术不仅仅用于战争。在和平年代,一些招式经过艺术化的加工,从而形成武术舞蹈,极具审美价值。

Driven by film and television works such as *Shaolin Temple* and a large number of excellent literary works, Shaolin Kung fu has become a household name in the mainstream wushu **category**⑥, and Shaolin Temple has become a Wulin sacred place in the people's hearts. In the

Southern and Northern dynasties, after his practice of facing the wall, **Bodhidharma**⑦ created the Shaolin Kung fu School, and after a long period of time and generations of Shaolin people's efforts, he formed a Wushu system, composed of boxing, stick-fighting, instrument routines, and so on.

在《少林寺》等影视作品和一大批优秀文学作品的带动下，少林功夫成为家喻户晓的主流武术类别，少林寺也成为人们心中的武林圣地。南北朝时期，达摩祖师经过面壁修行，创造了少林功夫派，经过漫长的岁月和一代代少林人的努力，形成了一个由拳术、棍法、器械套路等组成的武术体系。

Wushu pursues a kind of integrated concept of internal and external unity, which is not only to train the external healthy body, but also to pursue the internal mental fortitude and indomitable spirit. Wushu practitioners follow the moral requirements of respecting teachers, loving friends, observing etiquette and keeping faith, and acting bravely for a just cause, which is of great help to maintain social **prosperity**⑧ and stability.

武术追求内外合一的整体观念，既是为了练就外在健康的体魄，又追求内在心性的刚毅和顽强精神。练武者遵循敬师爱友、讲礼守信和见义勇为的道德要求，对维护社会繁荣稳定有极大帮助。

 佳句点睛 **Punchlines**

1. Taijiquan is a kind of healthy movement which shows the beauty of hardness and softness, displaying the charm of Chinese Kung fu.

太极拳是一招一式尽显刚柔相济之美、一动一静尽展中国功夫气韵的健康运动。

2. Wushu is a special way of sports explored by Chinese people in their long-term production and life, and also a measure of self-defense.

武术是中国人民在长期的生产和生活中探索出的一种特殊的运动方式,也是一种防身的手段。

3. Wushu performance is of high ornamental value. Whether it is a competitive performance routine or a **confrontational**① Sanda (free combat) competition, it not only gives people a beautiful experience, but also inspires and educates them by watching the power and skills displayed by the performers.

武术表演具有很高的观赏价值,无论是竞技性表演套路,还是对抗性散打比赛,通过观看表演者展示的功力和技巧,不仅给人以美的体验,还能使人受到启发和教育。

情景对话 Situational Dialogue

A: The holiday is coming. What's your plan for the weekend?

B: I have no idea yet, Jerry. I'd like to have a good rest.

A: Sounds good, but I've heard there's going to be a new movie named I*p Man 4* this Sunday.

B: Really? *Ip Man 4*. I started looking forward to this movie two months ago. There have been so many things recently that I have forgotten it. Do you also like Chinese Kung fu?

A: Yes, I like Chinese Kung fu very much. It is the essence of China. I like its routines. It's so cool! I know that *Ip Man* is a series of films, which is about the life and deeds of a great Wushu master, whose name is Ip Man. Wushu practitioners pursue peace and justice. They even risk their lives to defend their beliefs.

B: You're right. In that case, let's go see it together.

A: 假期就要来临了,你这周末有什么打算?

B: 还没想好,我想好好休息一下。

A: 是个好主意,不过我听说这周日会上映一场新电影《叶问4》,我想去看看。

B: 真的吗? 我两个月前就开始期待这部电影了,最近事情太多了,我竟然都忘记了。你也喜欢中国功夫吗?

A: 是的,我非常喜欢中国功夫,它是中国的国粹,我很喜欢里面

民俗文化

的招式，非常酷！我知道《叶问》是一部系列电影，它是关于一代武术大师叶问生平事迹的影片。武术人追求的是和平正义，他们甚至不惜用生命去捍卫自己的信仰。

B：你说得对。既然这样，我们就一起去看吧。

生词注解 Notes

① ancestor /ˈænsestə(r)/　　n. 祖先；始祖

② accumulate /əˈkjuːmjəleɪt/　　vt. 积累；积聚

③ lop /lɒp/　　vt. 砍伐；修剪

④ summarize /ˈsʌməraɪz/　　vt. 总结；概述

⑤ aesthetic /iːsˈθetɪk/　　adj. 审美的；美学的

⑥ category /ˈkætəɡərɪ/　　n. 种类；分类

⑦ Bodhidharma /ˌbɒdɪˈdɑːmə/　　n. 菩提达摩；达摩祖师

⑧ prosperity /prɒˈsperətɪ/　　n. 繁荣；成功

⑨ confrontational /ˌkɒnfrʌnˈteɪʃənl/　　adj. 对抗的；对抗性的

杂技

Acrobatics

导入语 Lead-in

　　杂技是指演员通过身体技巧完成一系列高难度动作的表演性节目。大约在新石器时代，原始人在休息娱乐时常常表演武技，这是杂技表演的前身。杂技在汉代称为"百戏"，隋唐时称为"散乐"，唐宋以后才称为"杂技"。杂技内容繁多、形式各异，包括力技、形体技巧、耍弄技巧、高空节目、柔术、口技、驯兽、变戏法等。中国著名的杂技之乡有河北的沧州吴桥、河南的濮阳、安徽的广德和湖北的天门等，这些地方的杂技表演都具有悠久的历史和深厚的群众基础。2007年，河北省吴桥县杂技团获得中国文化部首届文化遗产日奖。

文化剪影 Cultural Outline

Many of the events in the **acrobatic**① performance are the refinement of life skills, labor techniques and wushu skills. For the most part, performance props are living **utensils**② and labor tools, such as bowls, plates, ropes, poles, ladders and other common objects, which have become a magic weapon to create miracles in the hands of acrobats. Acrobatics has great adaptability, so whether in the splendid theater or in the open-air square in the countryside, the knowledgeable wise men or the **illiterate**③ vagabonds can feel the charm of acrobatics.

杂技表演中的很多项目是生活技能、劳动技术和武术技巧的提炼。表演道具大多是生活用具和劳动工具，如碗、盘、绳、杆、梯等常见物件，在杂技人的手中就成了创造奇迹的法宝。杂技具有极大的适应性，无论在金碧辉煌的剧场还是在农村的露天广场，无论是知识渊博的智者还是目不识丁的流浪汉，都可以感受到杂技的魅力。

Wuqiao in Cangzhou, Hebei is worthy of "The Hometown of Acrobatic". There is a popular **doggerel**④ among people there that "from an elderly of ninety-nine years old to a toddler, everyone has their own tricks of acrobatics in Wuqiao". It can be seen that acrobatics is very popular in Wuqiao. In 2007, Wuqiao Acrobatics was included in *The First Batch of National* **Intangible**⑤ *Cultural Heritage List* by the State Council.

技艺 第六部分

河北沧州吴桥县是当之无愧的"杂技之乡",民间流传着一段顺口溜"上至九十九,下至才会走,吴桥耍玩意,人人有一手"。由此可见,杂技在吴桥十分普及。2007年,吴桥杂技被国务院列入《第一批国家级非物质文化遗产名录》。

There have been many brilliant sparks between acrobatic arts and Chinese wine culture in the long history. Many acrobatic items are closely linked with the wine; acrobatic artists use their superb skills and masterly craftsmanship to achieve an organic combination of the two, bringing the audience a great **visual**⑥ enjoyment.

杂技艺术与中国酒文化在历史长河中碰撞出了绚烂的火花,很多杂技项目都和酒有着密切联系,杂技艺人以其高超的技巧和精湛的工匠精神实现了二者的有机结合,带给观众极大的视觉享受。

佳句点睛 Punchlines

1. Acrobatics, which is most famous for its thrill, **complexity**⑦ and high difficulty, is an art that challenges the limits of the body.

杂技大多以惊险、复杂和高难度而著称,是挑战超越身体极限的艺术。

2. Acrobatics inherits and carries forward the **essence**⑧ of tradi-tional art, but also with the development of the times innovates constantly and maintains a strong vitality.

杂技继承和发扬了传统艺术的精华,也随着时代发展不断创新,保持着顽强的生命力。

3. Chinese acrobatics has a strict tradition of learning from masters in succession, its skills handed down from generation to generation, so that every acrobat has the good quality of honouring teachers and esteeming the truth, and has consciously undertaken the historical mission of carrying forward the skills.

中国杂技具有严密的师承传统,技艺代代相传,每一位杂技人都具有尊师重道的美好品质,自觉承担着将技艺发扬光大的历史使命。

 情景对话 Situational Dialogue

A: I've heard that you went to Hebei for a travel some time ago. How did you like it?

B: Wonderful. It was really a memorable trip. The people there are very friendly, and there are a lot of yummy special snacks.

A: There are not only a lot of yummy food there, but also the acrobatics is also very famous. Did you go to see it?

B: Of course, the acrobats have very **flexible**⑨ bodies. I saw one actor holding the head of another with one hand, and then doing all kinds of breathtakingly difficult movements in midair.

A: Incredible⑩.

B: The people who watched on the scene stood up and cheered for them!

A: Behind these wonderful moments is their hard training.

B: That's right.

A: 我听说你前段时间去河北旅游了,感觉怎么样?

B: 非常好,那真是一次令人难忘的旅行!那里的人们非常友好,而且有很多美味可口的特色小吃。

A: 那里不仅有很多美食,而且杂技也非常有名。你去看了吗?

B: 当然了,杂技演员的身体非常柔韧,我看到一个演员单手扶着另一个演员的头,然后身体在半空中做着各种高难度动作。

A: 不可思议!

B: 当时观看的人们都站起来为他们欢呼!

A: 这些精彩瞬间的背后是他们的艰苦训练。

B: 说得没错。

生词注解 Notes

① acrobatic /ˌækrəˈbætɪk/ *adj.* 杂技的;特技的

② utensil /juːˈtensl/ *n.* 用具;器皿

③ illiterate /ɪˈlɪtərət/ *adj.* 文盲的;不识字的

④ doggerel /ˈdɒɡərəl/ *n.* 打油诗;顺口溜

⑤ intangible /ɪnˈtændʒəbl/ *adj.* 无形的;触摸不到的

⑥ visual /ˈvɪʒuəl/ *adj.* 视觉的；视力的

⑦ complexity /kəmˈpleksətɪ/ *n.* 复杂性；复杂错综的事物

⑧ essence /ˈesns/ *n.* 精华；本质

⑨ flexible /ˈfleksəbl/ *adj.* 灵活的；柔韧的

⑩ incredible /ɪnˈkredəbl/ *adj.* 难以置信的；极好的

围棋

Go

导入语 Lead-in

围棋,古称"弈",又称"坐隐""方圆""乌鹭""手谈""忘忧""黑白""星阵""围猎""鬼阵"等,是琴棋书画四大才艺之一。先秦典籍《世本·作篇》记载:"尧造围棋,丹朱善之"。相

传,为了使儿子丹朱回归正道,帝尧创造了围棋,希望他养成勤学善思的习惯。要在对弈中获胜,需讲究策略和技巧,这与战争有异曲同工之妙,因此围棋之战也成为培养军事人才的重要途径。围棋使用方格棋盘和黑白圆子对弈,盘面有纵横各19条等距离、垂直交叉的平行线,构成361个交叉点,以围地多者为胜。棋手等级包括段位和级位。古代围棋与现代围棋下法基本一样,区别就是前者以子多为胜。围棋被称为世界上最复杂的棋盘游戏。

文化剪影 Cultural Outline

Go (also known as Weiqi), which originated in China, was widely spread in the Spring and Autumn Period and the Warring States period. During the Sui and Tang dynasties, it was introduced into Japan through North Korea and then to European countries. The modern Go board is divided into three hundred and sixty-one **intersecting**① points by nineteen horizontal and **vertical**② lines. The black and white pieces move on the intersecting points **alternately**③. After the pieces are dropped, they cannot be moved. In the end, the one who seized more land would win the victory. Therefore, Go is also known as the ballet of black and white patterns interwoven on a chessboard.

围棋起源于中国,早在春秋战国时期就广泛流传。隋唐时期,围棋经朝鲜传入日本,而后传入欧洲各国。现代围棋棋盘上有横纵19条线将其分成361个交叉点,黑白棋子走在交叉点上,双方交替行棋,落子后不能移动,最终围地多者取胜。因此,围棋也被称为交织在棋盘上的黑白芭蕾。

During the Northern and Southern dynasties, there was a trend of **advocating**④ the theories of Lao Tzu and Zhuang Tzu, so Go was called "hand-talk" by the scholars and writers, and Go made **unprecedented**⑤ development. During the Tang and Song dynasties, there were many famous Go players in the delegations of foreign missions to

China while the game between the chess players became an important bridge of cultural exchanges between Chinese and foreign countries.

南北朝时期出现了一种崇尚老庄学说的思想潮流,文人墨客把下围棋称为"手谈",围棋得到了空前发展。唐宋时期,外国来华的使团里不乏围棋名手,而棋手间的对弈也成为中外文化交流的重要桥梁。

Go is of great help to the development of human brain intelligence, playing a positive role in **enhancing**⑥ people's memory, calculation and comprehensive judgment. In the meantime, there are many similarities between Go and economics, which studies how to reasonably **allocate**⑦ various scarce resources while Go studies how to let limited pieces control a larger board. From some point of view, Go resembles the enclosure movement in the economic history.

围棋对人脑智力的开发有极大的帮助,对增强人的记忆力、计算能力和综合判断力都能起到积极作用。同时,围棋与经济学有很多相似之处,经济学研究如何合理分配各种稀缺资源,围棋则是研究如何让有限的棋子掌控更大的棋盘。从某种角度来看,围棋类似经济史上的圈地运动。

佳句点睛　Punchlines

1. Go is recognized as the most complex board game in the world because its rules are simple, and the space of falling pieces is large,

which makes it changeable and attractive.

围棋规则简单，落子空间大，变化多端，魅力无穷，被公认为世界上最复杂的棋盘游戏。

2. There are nine stars on the board of Go, the middlemost one is called "Tianyuan", which means the highest point in the sky, and multiple **concentric**® squares can be found at the center.

围棋盘上有九颗星，最中间的被称为"天元"，意为天空最高点，以其为中心可以发现多个同心正方形。

3. Go has been compared to "a black-and-white world", which combines science, art and competition. Though it has developed for thousands of years, it is still flourishing and has become an international cultural competition.

围棋将科学、艺术和竞技融为一体，被喻为"黑白世界"，历经千年发展却仍长盛不衰，已经成为一种国际性文化竞技活动。

情景对话 Situational Dialogue

A: Look, what a fine day! Let's go out and play.

B: Great. Where would you like to go?

A: How about going to the Go club?

B: Go? Can you play it?

A: Yeah, I've been learning to play Go since my childhood. Can you play Go?

B: No, I won't, but I've read books about it. It is said that Go was invented by the Chinese thousands of years ago. Its rules are so simple, but there are a lot of **unpredictable**⑨ changes when we play it. In order to win, we must grasp the overall situation and adapt to the circumstances.

A: You're right. I think you should have a try.

B: Alright, let's go.

A:你看天气多好,我们一起出去玩吧。

B:好啊,你想去哪里?

A:去围棋社怎么样?

B:围棋? 你会下围棋?

A:是啊,我从小就开始学下围棋了。你会下围棋吗?

B:不,我不会,不过我看过相关的书,书上说围棋是几千年前中国人发明的,它的规则非常简单,但在下围棋时有很多难以预测的变化,要想胜出,需要有把握全局和随机应变的能力。

A:你说得对,我想你应该去尝试一下。

B:好,咱们走吧。

生词注解　Notes

① intersecting /ˌɪntəˈsektɪŋ/ *adj.* 交叉的;相交的

② vertical /ˈvɜːtɪkl/ *adj.* 垂直的;直立的

③ alternately /ɔːlˈtɜːnətlɪ/   adv. 交替地；轮流地

④ advocate /ˈædvəkət/   vt. 提倡；拥护

⑤ unprecedented /ʌnˈpresɪdentɪd/   adj. 空前的；前所未有的

⑥ enhance /ɪnˈhɑːns/   vt. 提高；加强

⑦ allocate /ˈæləkeɪt/   vt. 分配；拨出

⑧ concentric /kənˈsentrɪk/   adj. 同轴的；同心的

⑨ unpredictable /ˌʌnprɪˈdɪktəbl/   adj. 不可预测的；捉摸不透的

技艺 第六部分

相声

Crosstalk

导入语 Lead-in

　　相声是一种以说笑或滑稽问答引起观众发笑的民间说唱曲艺，表演形式是说、学、逗、唱，主要采用口头方式，如单口相声、对口相声、群口相声等。常用道具有折扇、手绢、醒木、桌子、竹板等。相声表演采取直接面向观众的方式，这种形式满足了广大观众的参与意识，大大加强了演员与观众的互动交流，具有独特的民族艺术魅力。著名的相声表演艺术家有马三立、侯宝林、马季、冯巩等，相声的代表剧目有《关公战秦琼》《买猴》《夜行记》《如此照相》等。

文化剪影　Cultural Outline

Originating in northern China during the Ming and Qing Dynasties, crosstalk is a kind of comedic dialogue, in which two persons use the Beijing dialect to fight back and forth in a humorous way. At present, crosstalk is **flourishing**① in Beijing, Tianjin, Hebei and other places, enjoying a high reputation at home and abroad.

相声源于明清时期的华北地区，是一种喜剧性的对话，两位表演者使用北京方言，以幽默的方式来回斗嘴，目前相声艺术在京津冀等地正蓬勃发展，在国内外享有盛誉。

Crosstalk is performed in the combination of speaking, imitating, teasing and singing. It mainly uses oral methods such as **stand-up**②, crosstalk and group crosstalk. Through vivid and rich desc-riptions of characters and events, it is intended to express the thought-provoking things behind the humor with representative actors including, Ma Sanli, Hou Baolin, and so on.

相声以说、学、逗、唱相结合的形式表演，主要采用单口相声、对口相声、群口相声等口头方式，通过生动丰富地描绘人物和事件，旨在表达幽默背后发人深省的东西，代表性的相声演员有马三立、侯宝林等。

The main **props**③ of crosstalk performance are folding fans, hand-kerchiefs, attention-catching block, and so on. Crosstalk is famous for its humor and **sarcasm**④, its theme originating from the life of the masses, and it raises and reflects the problems of the masses' concern, which is widely popular in the society.

相声表演的主要道具有折扇、手绢、醒木等。相声以幽默、讽刺著称，其主题来源于群众生活，提出并反映群众关心的问题，在社会上广受欢迎。

佳句点睛 Punchlines

1. Crosstalk is a kind of comedy dialogue, which is popular in Beijing, Tianjin and Hebei area and enjoys high reputation in the world.

相声是一种喜剧性的对话，流行于京津冀地区，在世界范围内享有盛誉。

2. Crosstalk is intended to express thought-provoking problems behind humor, which is of certain significance for social development.

相声意在表达幽默背后发人深省的问题，对社会发展具有一定的意义。

3. Crosstalk reveals the significant charm of China's local folk culture and wins the love of a large audience.

相声展示了中国本土民俗文化的巨大魅力，赢得了广大观众的喜爱。

情景对话　Situational Dialogue

A: Have you seen the programs of the Spring Festival **Gala**[5] of 2019? Which one impressed you most?

B: My favorite program is the crosstalk *Witty Repartee*[6] by Yue Yunpeng and Sun Yue. It is so funny and humorous that I love it very much.

A: Really wonderful. Crosstalk seems to appear on the spring festival gala stage every year. Can you explain more to me?

B: Sure. Crosstalk is a comedic dialogue, a classic form of Chinese folk art, in which two people, usually in Beijing **dialect**[7], engage in humorous teasing. What is more, crosstalk is a combination of speaking, imitating, teasing and singing, mainly adopting stand-up, counterpart crosstalk, group crosstalk, and so on, well received in North China.

A: After hearing your explanation, I have a better knowledge of crosstalk and cannot wait to appreciate more crosstalk performances.

B: I'm glad to hear that. The Crosstalk Programs known as *Happy Teahouse and Humorous Crosstalk Reality Show* are very popular recently. You can enjoy them online.

A: That's great. Many thanks.

B: Never mind.

A: 你看过2019年春节联欢晚会中的节目吗？哪一个对你印象

最深?

B: 我最喜欢的节目是岳云鹏和孙悦的相声《妙言趣语》。这个节目非常有趣和好笑,我非常喜欢它。

A: 的确很精彩。相声似乎每年都会出现在春节联欢晚会的舞台上。你能再给我多讲讲相声吗?

B: 当然可以。相声是一种喜剧性的对话,是中国传统民间艺术的一种经典形式,通常是两个人用北京方言以幽默的方式来回斗嘴。另外,相声是说、学、逗、唱的结合体,主要采用单口相声、对口相声和群口相声等,在华北地区颇受欢迎。

A: 听了你的解释,我对相声有了更好的了解,迫不及待地想欣赏更多的相声表演。

B: 我很高兴听到这些,《快乐茶馆》和《幽默相声真人秀》两档相声节目最近很流行,你可以在网上欣赏。

A: 太棒了!多谢。

B: 不客气。

生词注解 Notes

① flourishing /ˈflʌrɪʃɪŋ/ *adj.* 繁荣的;盛行的

② stand-up /ˈstændʌp/ *n.* 单口相声;单口喜剧

③ prop /prɒp/ *n.* 道具;支柱

④ sarcasm /ˈsɑːkæzəm/ *n.* 讽刺;挖苦

⑤ gala /ˈɡɑːlə/ *n.* 节日盛会

⑥ repartee /ˌrepɑːˈtiː/ *n.* 机敏的应答;妙语

⑦ dialect /ˈdaɪəlekt/ *n.* 方言;土话

秧歌

Yangko

导入语　Lead-in

秧歌，也称"扭秧歌"，是流传于中国北方地区的传统舞蹈类型，具有群众性、表演性和自娱性等特点。秧歌的起源与农业劳作有密切关系，据说古代农民在进行插秧、拔秧等农事劳动时用唱歌的形式减轻劳作之苦，舞蹈动作来自插秧时劳作的动作，经过艺术加工改编，逐渐形成集锣鼓、歌、舞等于一体的综合艺术。秧歌舞队一般由十几人到百余人组成，表演内容为中国历史故事和神话传说，表演方式为唱秧歌、扭秧歌、戏曲秧歌和戏剧秧歌。秧歌是中国农村流行的一种传统民间舞蹈，不仅是我国劳动人民群众宣泄情绪、表达感情的重要手段，也表达了人们节庆期间的愉悦心情和对美好生活的憧憬。2006年，秧歌被国务院列入《第一批国家级非物质文化遗产名录》。

文化剪影　Cultural Outline

Yangko is a traditional dance spread in northern China. Its origin is closely related to agricultural labor. Its action is to imitate the action of **transplanting**① rice **seedlings**②, thus forming the art form of the combination of song and dance at present.

秧歌是流传于中国北方的一种传统舞蹈。秧歌的起源与农业劳动密切相关。秧歌的动作是模仿插秧动作，从而形成了目前歌、舞相结合的艺术形式。

Yangko is based on the theme of Chinese historical stories and myths and legends, displaying traditional Chinese folk dances in the form of Yangko singing, dance, opera and drama, and expressing people's cheerful mood and **vision**③ for a better life.

秧歌是以中国历史故事和神话传说为主题，通过唱秧歌、扭秧歌、戏曲秧歌和戏剧秧歌等形式展示中国传统民间舞蹈，表达了人们愉快的心情和对美好生活的憧憬。

Yangko is a **comprehensive**④ art that combines gongs and drums, singing and dancing, and has the characteristics of mass, performance and self-entertainment. It is generally performed by the Yangko team, and each team is composed of ten to one hundred people.

秧歌是一种集锣鼓、歌舞于一体的综合性艺术，具有群体性、表演性和自娱性等特点，一般由秧歌队表演，每个队由十人到百人组成。

民俗文化

 佳句点睛　Punchlines

1. Yangko is a type of traditional Chinese dance closely related to agricultural labor.

秧歌是一种与农业劳动密切相关的中国传统舞蹈。

2. Yangko **conveys**⑤ people's joyful mood and longing for a better life during festivals.

秧歌舞蹈表达了人们节庆期间的快乐心情和对美好生活的向往。

3. Yangko is a public entertainment event embodying lively and cheerful atmosphere of traditional Chinese festival.

秧歌是一项能够体现中国传统节日轻松欢快气氛的公共娱乐活动。

 生词注解　Notes

① transplant /trænsˈplɑːnt/　*vt.* 移植；移栽

② seedling /ˈsiːdlɪŋ/　*n.* 秧苗；幼苗

③ vision /ˈvɪʒn/　*n.* 憧憬；愿景

④ comprehensive /ˌkɒmprɪˈhensɪv/　*adj.* 综合的；全部的

⑤ convey /kənˈveɪ/　*vt.* 传达；转达

高跷

Stilts

导入语 Lead-in

高跷,也称"踩高跷""扎高脚"或"走高腿",是盛行于中国北方的一种群众性技艺表演。高跷早在春秋时期便已出现,是一种技术性强、形式多样、生动活泼的中国传统民俗活动。据说,古代人为了采集树上的野果,在腿上绑上长棍,之后经过艺术加工,逐步发展为现在的"高跷"。高跷一般以舞队的形式表演,舞队人数由十几到数十不等,集体边舞边走,舞蹈者脚上绑着长木跷,扮演古代神话和历史故事中的某个角色形象,表演优美生动、幽默惊险,颇受观众喜爱。高跷由民间的锣鼓乐队伴奏,这种民间舞蹈活动不仅丰富了人民群众的精神文化生活,也体现了老百姓过节时喜庆热闹的氛围和祈盼来年风调雨顺、五谷丰登的美好愿望。2006年，高跷被国务院列入《第一批国家级非物质文化遗产名录》。

文化剪影　Cultural Outline

Stilts①, also known as "Walking on Stilts", which can be traced back to the Spring and Autumn Period, is popular in northern China as a traditional folk dance. According to the legend, when the ancients gathered wild fruits on the trees, they would tie their legs with long sticks. After artistic processing, this kind of labor has gradually developed into the present stilts.

高跷，又称"踩高跷"，最早可追溯到春秋时期，是中国北方流行的一种传统民间舞蹈。传说，古人采集树上野果时常常用长棍绑在腿上，这种劳动方式经过艺术加工，逐渐发展成为现在的高跷。

Walking on stilts is a common **recreational**② activity in rural China, which can be divided into **civil**③ stilts and **martial**④ stilts. Civil stilts refers to playing roles in traditional dramas such as *Journey to the West* and *The Legend of the White Snake*; and martial stilts refers to performing **stunts**⑤ that people expect, such as rising high into the air, rolling, and so on. These performances would add a relaxed and cheerful atmosphere to people's spiritual and cultural life.

踩高跷是中国农村一种常见的娱乐活动，可分为文跷和武跷：文跷是指扮演《西游记》《白蛇传》等传统剧目中的角色；武跷是指人们期待的绝技表演,如腾空、翻滚等,这些表演为人们的精神文化生活增添了轻松欢乐的氛围。

Performers use all kinds of props to integrate dance, performance, drama and **acrobatics**⑥. The program is unusually brilliant and breathtaking, showcasing the festive atmosphere of people celebrating the festival and looking forward to a better future.

演员们运用各种道具,集舞蹈、表演、戏剧、杂技于一体,节目精彩纷呈、惊心动魄,呈现出人民群众欢度佳节、憧憬美好未来的喜庆气氛。

佳句点睛　Punchlines

1. Stilts is a traditional Chinese folk dance, whose performing art is characterized by the features of masses and techniques.

高跷是中国传统民间舞蹈,其表演艺术具有群众性和技巧性。

2. Stilts is a kind of leisure activity, which enriches people's daily cultural life.

高跷是一种休闲活动,丰富了人们日常的文化生活。

3. Stilts is a comprehensive activity that shows the unique regional culture of the local people.

高跷是一项综合性活动,展示了当地人民独特的地域文化。

生词注解 Notes

① stilt /stɪlt/ n. 高跷；支柱

② recreational /ˌrekrɪˈeɪʃənl/ adj. 娱乐的；消遣的

③ civil /ˈsɪvl/ adj. 文明的；民用的

④ martial /ˈmɑːʃl/ adj. 军事的；尚武的

⑤ stunt /stʌnt/ n. 绝技；噱头

⑥ acrobatics /ˌækrəˈbætɪks/ n. 杂技；巧妙手法

腰鼓舞

Waist Drum Dance

导入语 Lead-in

腰鼓舞，也称"打腰鼓"，流传于陕北安塞县一带，是一种在中国广泛流行的民间舞蹈。腰鼓起源于古代的战鼓，每当遇到困难、危险或取胜时，古代边关战士都要腰系战鼓并击鼓报警、助威、求援或庆祝胜利。经过艺术加工，演变成了现在的腰鼓舞。腰鼓舞是一种集体舞蹈，主要表达欢乐喜庆的气氛。腰鼓队人员少则四到八人，多则十到上百人。舞者腰间系一面椭圆形小鼓，双手各持一只鼓槌，边打边舞，舞步变化多端，能走出各种漂亮图案。腰鼓队表演时，舞者慷慨激昂，动作整齐，场面壮观，声势浩大，令人振奋。

民俗文化

文化剪影　Cultural Outline

Waist Drum Dance is a popular traditional Chinese dance in Ansai County, Shaanxi Province. In ancient times, when faced with danger, difficulty or victory, soldiers would use their waist drums to sound an alarm, ask for help, or celebrate victory in the war. After a long period of **evolution**①, it **eventually**② developed into the present waist drum.

腰鼓舞是陕西省安塞县流行的一种中国传统舞蹈。在古代,每当遇到危险、困难或取胜时,士兵们都会利用腰鼓发出警报、请求帮助或庆祝战争胜利。经过长期演变,最终发展成为现在的腰鼓舞。

Ansai Waist Drum Dance and Luochuan Waist Drum Dance of Shaanxi are well-known. There are many performers, and the number of performers **ranges**③ from four to eight or ten to hundreds. During large-scale events or festivals, dancers are tied with an **oval**④ drum around their waists, holding drumsticks in their hands and jumping while playing to express the joy of festivals.

陕西安塞腰鼓舞和洛川腰鼓舞声名显赫。表演者数量众多,表演队伍人数为四至八人或十至数百人不等。在大型活动或节日期间,舞者腰间绑着一面椭圆形鼓,双手持鼓槌,边舞边打,以表达节日的快乐。

Waist Drum Dance is a kind of collective dance with distinctive features. During the performance, the dancers are passionate, bold and orderly. They can create all kinds of beautiful **patterns**⑤ through changing dance steps. The scene is **spectacular**⑥ and magnificent, aiming at blessing the crops and the common people.

腰鼓舞是一种具有鲜明特色的集体舞蹈。表演时，舞者激情澎湃、豪放有序，可以通过变幻的舞步走出各种漂亮图案，场面恢宏壮观，旨在为庄稼和百姓祈福。

佳句点睛 Punchlines

1. Waist Drum Dance embodies the military function in the ancient battlefields.

腰鼓舞在古代战场中发挥着军事功能。

2. Waist Drum Dance expresses people's wisdom of collectivism and the joy of festivals.

腰鼓舞表达了人们集体主义的智慧和节日的快乐。

3. Waist Drum Dance is a kind of entertainment that reflects the unique local culture of traditional Chinese festivals.

腰鼓舞是一种体现中国传统节日中独特地方文化的娱乐活动。

情景对话 Situational Dialogue

A: Did you see the National Day Gala last night? What's your impression on the waist drum dance?

B: Oh, Waist Drum Dance is a type of traditional Chinese dance popular in Ansai County, northern Shaanxi Province. During the big events or festivals, the dancers are tied with an oval drum at the waist, holding a drumstick in both hands, dancing while playing to express their joyful feeling and festival enjoyment.

A: Superb. What else do you know about other forms of traditional Chinese dances?

B: Yes, I do. Actually, traditional Chinese dances are a kind of collective dance with characteristics of masses, performance and self-entertainment. Apart from waist drum dance, stilt-walking, Yangko, lion dance, and so on, are all traditional Chinese folk dances revealing people's wisdom of collectivism and the joy of festivals.

A: After hearing your explanation, I have a better knowledge of the traditional Chinese folk dance.

B: I suggest you go to the local countryside in the northern part of China during the Spring Festival to enjoy the **authentic**⑦ local performance.

A: 你看昨天的国庆联欢晚会了吗？你对腰鼓舞印象如何？

B: 噢,腰鼓舞是陕西省安塞县流行的一种中国传统舞蹈。在大型活动或节日期间,舞者腰间绑着一面椭圆形鼓,双手持鼓槌,边舞边打,以表达节日的快乐心情和幸福感受。

A: 太棒了!你还知道其他形式的中国传统舞蹈吗?

B: 知道。实际上,中国传统舞蹈是一种集群众性、表演性、自娱性于一身的集体舞蹈。除了腰鼓舞、高跷舞、秧歌舞、狮子舞之外还有许多中国传统民间舞蹈,都体现了人们集体主义的智慧和节日的快乐。

A: 听了你的讲解,我中国传统舞蹈有了更好的了解。

B: 我建议你在春节期间到中国北方的乡村去欣赏正宗的本地演出。

生词注解 Notes

① evolution /ˌiːvəˈluːʃn/ *n.* 演变;进化

② eventually /ɪˈventʃuəli/ *adv.* 最后;终于

③ range /reɪndʒ/ *vi.* (在……内)变动

④ oval /ˈəʊvl/ *adj.* 椭圆形的;卵形的

⑤ pattern /ˈpætn/ *n.* 图案;模式

⑥ spectacular /spekˈtækjələ(r)/ *adj.* 壮观的;壮丽的

⑦ authentic /ɔːˈθentɪk/ *adj.* 真正的;真实的

民俗文化

皮影戏

Shadow Puppetry

导入语　Lead-in

皮影戏，又称"影子戏"或"灯影戏"，最早诞生于西汉时期，是一种历史悠久、影响广泛的中国民间艺术形式。皮影是指皮影戏中民间艺人用手工刀雕彩绘而成的皮制品，即以兽皮或纸板做成的人物剪影。观众通过白色幕布观看平面人偶表演的灯影。表演时，艺人们在操纵戏曲人物的同时采用当地流行的曲调讲述故事，并配以打击乐器和弦乐，形成了深受人们喜爱、具有浓厚乡土气息的民间艺术形式。皮影戏题材丰富，风格多样，新颖独特，充分体现了中国民间艺术的丰厚底蕴和民间艺人的聪明才智。2011年，皮影戏被联合国教科文组织列入《人类非物质文化遗产代表作名录》。

文化剪影　Cultural Outline

Shadow **puppetry**① is a form of Chinese folk art with a long history and far-reaching influence, which aims to tell the story by using **opaque**② characters to create the illusion of motion in front of an **illuminated**③ background. Influenced by many factors, it has developed into a variety of artistic styles.

皮影戏是一种具有悠久历史和深远影响的中国民间艺术形式，旨在利用不透明的人物形象，在灯光的映衬下，产生画面运动的幻觉，进行故事讲述。受多种因素的影响，皮影戏已经发展成多种风格的艺术形式。

Shadow puppetry is a representative of the traditional Chinese folk art, with its rich themes, **diverse**④ styles, and **novelty**⑤, which fully reflects the richness of the Chinese folk art and the wisdom of folk artists.

皮影戏是中国传统民间艺术的代表，它题材丰富，风格多样，新颖独特，充分体现了中国民间艺术的丰厚底蕴和民间艺人的聪明才智。

The development of shadow puppetry is a process of constant adjustment and **fusion**⑥, with a strong Chinese folk art. Shadow puppetry, often accompanied by drums and strings, has paved the way for

the appearance of modern films and movie cartoons.

皮影戏具有浓郁的中国民间艺术气息，它的发展是一个不断调整和融合的过程，皮影戏表演通常用打击乐器和弦乐伴奏，为现代电影和卡通电影的出现铺平了道路。

 ## 佳句点睛 Punchlines

1. Shadow puppetry embodies the richness of Chinese folk art and folk artists' **intelligence**⑦.

皮影戏体现了中国民间艺术的丰厚底蕴和民间艺人的聪明才智。

2. Shadow puppetry owns various styles with a strong local **flavor**⑧.

皮影戏风格多样，具有浓郁的地方特色。

3. Shadow puppetry has had a far-reaching influence on the invention of modern movies.

皮影对现代电影的发明产生了深远的影响。

 ## 情景对话 Situational Dialogue

A: Next week our school will hold a weekend party for the international students. What will your talent show be?

技艺

B: I'll perform shadow puppetry, which is a form of Chinese folk art with a time-honored history and far-reaching influence.

A: Bravo! Can you explain it to me in more detail?

B: Yes, I can. Shadow puppetry uses opaque figures to create the illusion of moving images against the light, making the story more dramatic, reflecting the richness of the Chinese folk art and the **ingenuity**⑨ of folk artists, and paving the way for the emergence of modern film and **animation**⑩.

A: Really wonderful. After hearing your explanation, I can't wait to see your performance.

B: I'm not well prepared now and need more time to practice performing it.

A: Practice makes perfect. Best wishes to you next weekend.

B: Thanks.

A: 下周我们学校将为国际学生举行周末聚会。你的才艺表演是什么?

B: 我要表演皮影戏,这是一种中国民间的艺术形式,它历史悠久,影响深远。

A: 太棒了。你能给我详细解释一下吗?

B: 能。皮影戏是利用不透明的人物形象,在灯光的映衬下,产生画面运动的幻觉,使故事情节化,充分体现了中国民间艺术的丰富性和民间艺术家的聪明才智,为现代电影和卡通电影的出现铺平了道路。

A: 真了不起。听了你的解释,我等不及要看你的表演了。

B: 我现在还没有准备好,需要更多时间来练习。

A: 熟能生巧。祝你下周末一切顺利。

B: 谢谢。

 生词注解 Notes

① puppetry /ˈpʌpɪtri/ n. 木偶戏

② opaque /əʊˈpeɪk/ adj. 不透明的;模糊的

③ illuminated /ɪˈluːmɪneɪtɪd/ adj. 被照亮的;被照明的

④ diverse /daɪˈvɜːs/ adj. 多种多样的;形形色色的

⑤ novelty /ˈnɒvltɪ/ n. 新奇;新奇的事物

⑥ fusion /ˈfjuːʒn/ n. 融合;熔化

⑦ intelligence /ɪnˈtelɪdʒəns/ n. 智慧;智力

⑧ flavor /ˈfleɪvə(r)/ n. 风味;滋味

⑨ ingenuity /ˌɪndʒəˈnjuːətɪ/ n. 心灵手巧;足智多谋

⑩ animation /ˌænɪˈmeɪʃn/ n. 动画制作;动画片

泥塑

Clay Sculpture

 导入语　Lead-in

　　天津泥人张彩塑创始于清代道光年间，创始人张长林心灵手巧，富有想象力，凭借较强的思辨能力和敏锐的观察能力，创作出一万多件栩栩如生、形象逼真、色彩丰富的艺术作品，在中国传统民间手工艺史上占有重要地位。其艺术作品不仅继承了传统泥塑艺术，而且从绘画、戏曲、剪纸等艺术形式中吸收营养，形成了独特风格，深受百姓喜爱，被亲切地称为"泥人张"。泥人张彩塑题材广泛，主要取材于民间故事、神话传说、舞台戏剧、文学名著和现实生活等，主题内容贴近生活，具有鲜明的地域特色。彩塑的艺术特点是"塑造"和"绘色"的结合，先塑造，后绘色，塑造出形神兼备、形象逼真、生活气息浓厚的艺术作品，在国内外享有盛誉。

 文化剪影 Cultural Outline

Clay Figurine Zhang is mainly popular in northern China. Founder Zhang Changlin is quick-witted and imaginative. His works not only inherit the traditional clay sculpture art, but also absorb the essence and **nutrition**① of painting, opera, paper-cut and other art forms, nicknamed as "Clay Figurine Zhang".

泥人张主要流行于中国北方地区,创始人张长林思维敏捷,富有想象力,他的作品不仅继承了传统泥塑艺术,而且吸收了绘画、戏曲、剪纸等其他艺术形式的精华和营养,被昵称为"泥人张"。

Clay Figurine Zhang is based on a wide range of materials, including **folklore**②, myths and legends, stage plays, literary classics and real life. Zhang Changlin has created more than ten thousand lifelike and colorful works of art with his strong ability of thinking and observation, which plays an important role in the history of traditional Chinese folk crafts.

泥人张取材广泛,包括民间故事、神话传说、舞台剧、文学名著和现实生活等。张长林以较强的思辨能力和敏锐的观察能力创作了一万多件栩栩如生、生动多彩的艺术作品,在中国传统民间工艺史上占有重要地位。

The theme of Clay Figurine Zhang is close to life, with distinct regional features. Its artistic feature is the combination of "shaping" and "painting", which creates works of art with both shape and spirit, lifelike image and strong flavor of life, enjoying high reputation at home and abroad.

泥人张题材贴近生活,具有鲜明的地域特色,其艺术特点是"形"与"画"相结合。泥人张作品形神兼备、形象逼真、生活气息浓厚,在国内外享有盛誉。

佳句点睛　Punchlines

1. Clay Figurine Zhang has inherited and carried forward the art of traditional clay sculpture.

泥人张继承和发扬了传统泥塑艺术。

2. Clay Figurine Zhang plays a **crucial**③ role in the history of traditional Chinese folk crafts.

泥人张在中国传统民间工艺史上占有重要地位。

3. Clay Figurine Zhang is close to life, with distinct regional characteristics, enjoying a high reputation at home and abroad.

泥人张作品贴近生活,具有鲜明的地域特色,在国内外享有盛誉。

生词注解　Notes

① nutrition /njuˈtrɪʃn/　n. 营养;营养品
② folklore /ˈfəʊklɔː(r)/　n. 民间传说;民间风俗
③ crucial /ˈkruːʃl/　adj. 重要的;决定性的

老北京兔儿爷

Old Beijing Rabbit Figurine

 导入语　Lead-in

老北京兔儿爷是用泥巴捏成的，兔首人身，姿态各异，最典型的形态是竖着两只大耳朵。兔儿爷的形象来自月亮上的玉兔，最早出现在明末，用来祭月，现在演变为融祭祀、娱乐于一体的汉族传统手工艺品，是北京代表性的非物质文化遗产之一。兔儿爷一般被定义为平安守护神，可以消灾避难，给人们带来好运和吉祥。因此，每逢过年过节或重大喜事，北京家家户户都会请一尊新兔儿爷回家，以表达对美好事物的祝福和期许，这种行为已经演变成北京人的一种传统习俗，目前老北京兔儿爷已经成为北京的形象大使和代表性的对外交流文化礼品之一。

文化剪影　Cultural Outline

　　The Old Beijing Rabbit Figurine, a clay figure of rabbit that appeared at the end of the Ming Dynasty, was used to worship the moon. It has developed into a traditional Han **handicraft**① that combines sacrifice and entertainment, and is one of the representative **intangible**② cultural heritages in Beijing.

　　老北京兔儿爷是明末出现的一种泥制兔俑,用于祭月,现已发展成为融祭祀、娱乐于一体的汉族传统手工艺品,是北京代表性的非物质文化遗产之一。

　　Old Beijing Rabbit Figurine was once used as the symbol of the Mid-Autumn Festival in Beijing. It is generally defined as a guardian of peace, which can **eliminate**③ disasters and bring good luck, health, peace and blessings to people. At present, Old Beijing Rabbit Figurine has become Beijing's image **ambassador**④ and one of the representative foreign exchange cultural gifts.

　　老北京兔儿爷曾被北京人视为中秋节的标志,一般被定义为平安的守护者,可以消灾避难,给人们带来好运、健康、平安和祝福。目前,老北京兔儿爷已经成为北京的形象大使和代表性的对外交流文化礼品之一。

　　The image of Old Beijing Rabbit Figurine derived from the Jade

Rabbit on the moon. Its head resembles a human head, with two large ears and different **postures**⑤. During the Spring Festival, every family in Beijing invites a new rabbit figurine to express their wishes and hopes for good things. This has evolved into a traditional custom of Beijing people.

老北京兔儿爷的形象源自月亮上的玉兔,它的头部仿照人的头部,竖着两只大耳朵,姿势各异。春节期间,北京家家户户都会请一尊新兔儿爷回家,来表达对美好事物的愿望和期许,这已经演变成北京人的一种传统习俗。

 ## 佳句点睛 Punchlines

1. Old Beijing Rabbit Figurine is a traditional handicraft of Han nationality integrating sacrifices and amusement functions.

老北京兔儿爷是融祭祀和娱乐功能于一体的汉族传统工艺品。

2. Rabbit Figurine is the image ambassador and one of the most representative foreign exchange cultural gift of Beijing.

兔儿爷是北京的形象大使和代表性的对外交流文化礼物之一。

3. Old Beijing Rabbit Figurine is used by people to express their wishes and expectations for the wonderful things and this has evolved into a traditional custom of Beijing people.

人们用老北京兔儿爷来表达对美好事物的愿望和期许,这已经演变成北京人的一种传统习俗。

情景对话 Situational Dialogue

A: How do you spend your weekend next week?

B: I plan to go to a clay sculpture shop to make a clay as a birthday present for my sister.

A: Sounds amazing. Can you offer more details about the clay sculpture culture?

B: Clay Sculpture Art reflects the wisdom of folk artists and is a treasure of traditional Chinese folk art, with strong regional characteristics, among which the most famous are Clay Figurine Zhang in Tianjin, Old Beijing Rabbit Figurine and Huishan Clay Figurine in Wuxi.

A: Really good. I go to Beijing frequently. Can you introduce more about Old Beijing Rabbit Figurine?

B: It is a traditional Han handicraft with sacrificial and entertainment functions, as one of the representative intangible cultural heritage in Beijing. If you go to Beijing next time, be sure to see Old Beijing Rabbit Figurine.

A: Sure, I was impressed by the charm of traditional Chinese folk art. Can I go together with you to have a look in person next weekend?

B: Yes, you can. Let's set off at eight o'clock in the morning, shall we?

A: That's great. See you there.

B: OK. See you there.

A: 下周末你怎么过啊?

B: 我打算去一家泥塑店做泥塑,作为送给妹妹的生日礼物。

A: 听起来不错。你能详细讲解一下泥塑文化吗?

B: 泥塑艺术反映了民间艺人智慧的结晶,是中国传统民间艺术的瑰宝,具有浓郁的地域特色,其中最著名的有天津泥人张、老北京兔儿爷和无锡惠山泥人。

A: 真好。我经常去北京,你能再讲讲老北京兔儿爷吗?

B: 老北京兔儿爷是具有祭祀和娱乐功能的汉族传统工艺品,是北京代表性的非物质文化遗产之一。如果你下次去北京,一定要去看老北京兔儿爷。

A: 当然,我非常喜爱中国传统民间艺术的魅力。下周末我能和你一起去看看吗?

B: 能。我们早上八点出发,好吗?

A: 太好了! 不见不散。

B: 行,不见不散。

 生词注解 Notes

① handicraft /ˈhændɪkrɑːft/ *n.* 手工艺;手工艺品

② intangible /ɪnˈtændʒəbl/ *adj.* 无形的;难以确定的

③ eliminate /ɪˈlɪmɪneɪt/ *vt.* 消除;清除

④ ambassador /æmˈbæsədə(r)/ *n.* 大使;使节

⑤ posture /ˈpɒstʃə(r)/ *n.* 姿势;态度